C-2197   CAREER EXAMINATION SERIES

This is your
PASSBOOK for...

Bus Driver

Test Preparation Study Guide
Questions & Answers

NATIONAL LEARNING CORPORATION®

COPYRIGHT NOTICE

This book is SOLELY intended for, is sold ONLY to, and its use is RESTRICTED to individual, bona fide applicants or candidates who qualify by virtue of having seriously filed applications for appropriate license, certificate, professional and/or promotional advancement, higher school matriculation, scholarship, or other legitimate requirements of education and/or governmental authorities.

This book is NOT intended for use, class instruction, tutoring, training, duplication, copying, reprinting, excerption, or adaptation, etc., by:

1) Other publishers
2) Proprietors and/or Instructors of "Coaching" and/or Preparatory Courses
3) Personnel and/or Training Divisions of commercial, industrial, and governmental organizations
4) Schools, colleges, or universities and/or their departments and staffs, including teachers and other personnel
5) Testing Agencies or Bureaus
6) Study groups which seek by the purchase of a single volume to copy and/or duplicate and/or adapt this material for use by the group as a whole without having purchased individual volumes for each of the members of the group
7) Et al.

Such persons would be in violation of appropriate Federal and State statutes.

PROVISION OF LICENSING AGREEMENTS – Recognized educational, commercial, industrial, and governmental institutions and organizations, and others legitimately engaged in educational pursuits, including training, testing, and measurement activities, may address request for a licensing agreement to the copyright owners, who will determine whether, and under what conditions, including fees and charges, the materials in this book may be used them. In other words, a licensing facility exists for the legitimate use of the material in this book on other than an individual basis. However, it is asseverated and affirmed here that the material in this book CANNOT be used without the receipt of the express permission of such a licensing agreement from the Publishers. Inquiries re licensing should be addressed to the company, attention rights and permissions department.

All rights reserved, including the right of reproduction in whole or in part, in any form or by any means, electronic or mechanical, including photocopying, recording, or by any information storage and retrieval system, without permission in writing from the Publisher.

Copyright © 2024 by
National Learning Corporation

212 Michael Drive, Syosset, NY 11791
(516) 921-8888 • www.passbooks.com
E-mail: info@passbooks.com

PUBLISHED IN THE UNITED STATES OF AMERICA

PASSBOOK® SERIES

THE *PASSBOOK® SERIES* has been created to prepare applicants and candidates for the ultimate academic battlefield – the examination room.

At some time in our lives, each and every one of us may be required to take an examination – for validation, matriculation, admission, qualification, registration, certification, or licensure.

Based on the assumption that every applicant or candidate has met the basic formal educational standards, has taken the required number of courses, and read the necessary texts, the *PASSBOOK® SERIES* furnishes the one special preparation which may assure passing with confidence, instead of failing with insecurity. Examination questions – together with answers – are furnished as the basic vehicle for study so that the mysteries of the examination and its compounding difficulties may be eliminated or diminished by a sure method.

This book is meant to help you pass your examination provided that you qualify and are serious in your objective.

The entire field is reviewed through the huge store of content information which is succinctly presented through a provocative and challenging approach – the question-and-answer method.

A climate of success is established by furnishing the correct answers at the end of each test.

You soon learn to recognize types of questions, forms of questions, and patterns of questioning. You may even begin to anticipate expected outcomes.

You perceive that many questions are repeated or adapted so that you can gain acute insights, which may enable you to score many sure points.

You learn how to confront new questions, or types of questions, and to attack them confidently and work out the correct answers.

You note objectives and emphases, and recognize pitfalls and dangers, so that you may make positive educational adjustments.

Moreover, you are kept fully informed in relation to new concepts, methods, practices, and directions in the field.

You discover that you are actually taking the examination all the time: you are preparing for the examination by "taking" an examination, not by reading extraneous and/or supererogatory textbooks.

In short, this PASSBOOK®, used directedly, should be an important factor in helping you to pass your test.

BUS DRIVER

DUTIES AND RESPONSIBILITIES
Drives a bus in accordance with law and rules and regulations of the transit authority. Collects fares. Cares for passengers' safety. Makes proper reports regarding revenues, accidents, inoperative or faulty equipment, and unusual occurrences. Cares for and protects the assigned vehicle. Performs related duties.

TESTS
The written test will be of the multiple-choice type and may include questions on: awareness of proper work attitudes, courtesy, responsibilities of transit employee in dealing with the public, and general responsibilities in handling municipal property; ability to read and interpret instructions and bulletins on rapid transit operations and rules and regulations; awareness of safety and defensive driving concepts in transit operations; ability to read and interpret basic transit schedules; ability to read and interpret transit route maps and to select proper transfer points and best route; arithmetic; and other related areas.

HOW TO TAKE A TEST

I. YOU MUST PASS AN EXAMINATION

A. WHAT EVERY CANDIDATE SHOULD KNOW

Examination applicants often ask us for help in preparing for the written test. What can I study in advance? What kinds of questions will be asked? How will the test be given? How will the papers be graded?

As an applicant for a civil service examination, you may be wondering about some of these things. Our purpose here is to suggest effective methods of advance study and to describe civil service examinations.

Your chances for success on this examination can be increased if you know how to prepare. Those "pre-examination jitters" can be reduced if you know what to expect. You can even experience an adventure in good citizenship if you know why civil service exams are given.

B. WHY ARE CIVIL SERVICE EXAMINATIONS GIVEN?

Civil service examinations are important to you in two ways. As a citizen, you want public jobs filled by employees who know how to do their work. As a job seeker, you want a fair chance to compete for that job on an equal footing with other candidates. The best-known means of accomplishing this two-fold goal is the competitive examination.

Exams are widely publicized throughout the nation. They may be administered for jobs in federal, state, city, municipal, town or village governments or agencies.

Any citizen may apply, with some limitations, such as the age or residence of applicants. Your experience and education may be reviewed to see whether you meet the requirements for the particular examination. When these requirements exist, they are reasonable and applied consistently to all applicants. Thus, a competitive examination may cause you some uneasiness now, but it is your privilege and safeguard.

C. HOW ARE CIVIL SERVICE EXAMS DEVELOPED?

Examinations are carefully written by trained technicians who are specialists in the field known as "psychological measurement," in consultation with recognized authorities in the field of work that the test will cover. These experts recommend the subject matter areas or skills to be tested; only those knowledges or skills important to your success on the job are included. The most reliable books and source materials available are used as references. Together, the experts and technicians judge the difficulty level of the questions.

Test technicians know how to phrase questions so that the problem is clearly stated. Their ethics do not permit "trick" or "catch" questions. Questions may have been tried out on sample groups, or subjected to statistical analysis, to determine their usefulness.

Written tests are often used in combination with performance tests, ratings of training and experience, and oral interviews. All of these measures combine to form the best-known means of finding the right person for the right job.

II. HOW TO PASS THE WRITTEN TEST

A. NATURE OF THE EXAMINATION

To prepare intelligently for civil service examinations, you should know how they differ from school examinations you have taken. In school you were assigned certain definite pages to read or subjects to cover. The examination questions were quite detailed and usually emphasized memory. Civil service exams, on the other hand, try to discover your present ability to perform the duties of a position, plus your potentiality to learn these duties. In other words, a civil service exam attempts to predict how successful you will be. Questions cover such a broad area that they cannot be as minute and detailed as school exam questions.

In the public service similar kinds of work, or positions, are grouped together in one "class." This process is known as *position-classification*. All the positions in a class are paid according to the salary range for that class. One class title covers all of these positions, and they are all tested by the same examination.

B. FOUR BASIC STEPS

1) Study the announcement

How, then, can you know what subjects to study? Our best answer is: "Learn as much as possible about the class of positions for which you've applied." The exam will test the knowledge, skills and abilities needed to do the work.

Your most valuable source of information about the position you want is the official exam announcement. This announcement lists the training and experience qualifications. Check these standards and apply only if you come reasonably close to meeting them.

The brief description of the position in the examination announcement offers some clues to the subjects which will be tested. Think about the job itself. Review the duties in your mind. Can you perform them, or are there some in which you are rusty? Fill in the blank spots in your preparation.

Many jurisdictions preview the written test in the exam announcement by including a section called "Knowledge and Abilities Required," "Scope of the Examination," or some similar heading. Here you will find out specifically what fields will be tested.

2) Review your own background

Once you learn in general what the position is all about, and what you need to know to do the work, ask yourself which subjects you already know fairly well and which need improvement. You may wonder whether to concentrate on improving your strong areas or on building some background in your fields of weakness. When the announcement has specified "some knowledge" or "considerable knowledge," or has used adjectives like "beginning principles of…" or "advanced … methods," you can get a clue as to the number and difficulty of questions to be asked in any given field. More questions, and hence broader coverage, would be included for those subjects which are more important in the work. Now weigh your strengths and weaknesses against the job requirements and prepare accordingly.

3) Determine the level of the position

Another way to tell how intensively you should prepare is to understand the level of the job for which you are applying. Is it the entering level? In other words, is this the position in which beginners in a field of work are hired? Or is it an intermediate or advanced level? Sometimes this is indicated by such words as "Junior" or "Senior" in the class title. Other jurisdictions use Roman numerals to designate the level – Clerk I, Clerk II, for example. The word "Supervisor" sometimes appears in the title. If the level is not indicated by the title, check the description of duties. Will you be working under very close supervision, or will you have responsibility for independent decisions in this work?

4) Choose appropriate study materials

Now that you know the subjects to be examined and the relative amount of each subject to be covered, you can choose suitable study materials. For beginning level jobs, or even advanced ones, if you have a pronounced weakness in some aspect of your training, read a modern, standard textbook in that field. Be sure it is up to date and has general coverage. Such books are normally available at your library, and the librarian will be glad to help you locate one. For entry-level positions, questions of appropriate difficulty are chosen – neither highly advanced questions, nor those too simple. Such questions require careful thought but not advanced training.

If the position for which you are applying is technical or advanced, you will read more advanced, specialized material. If you are already familiar with the basic principles of your field, elementary textbooks would waste your time. Concentrate on advanced textbooks and technical periodicals. Think through the concepts and review difficult problems in your field.

These are all general sources. You can get more ideas on your own initiative, following these leads. For example, training manuals and publications of the government agency which employs workers in your field can be useful, particularly for technical and professional positions. A letter or visit to the government department involved may result in more specific study suggestions, and certainly will provide you with a more definite idea of the exact nature of the position you are seeking.

III. KINDS OF TESTS

Tests are used for purposes other than measuring knowledge and ability to perform specified duties. For some positions, it is equally important to test ability to make adjustments to new situations or to profit from training. In others, basic mental abilities not dependent on information are essential. Questions which test these things may not appear as pertinent to the duties of the position as those which test for knowledge and information. Yet they are often highly important parts of a fair examination. For very general questions, it is almost impossible to help you direct your study efforts. What we can do is to point out some of the more common of these general abilities needed in public service positions and describe some typical questions.

1) General information

Broad, general information has been found useful for predicting job success in some kinds of work. This is tested in a variety of ways, from vocabulary lists to questions about current events. Basic background in some field of work, such as sociology or economics, may be sampled in a group of questions. Often these are principles which have become familiar to most persons through exposure rather than through formal training. It is difficult to advise you how to study for these questions; being alert to the world around you is our best suggestion.

2) Verbal ability

An example of an ability needed in many positions is verbal or language ability. Verbal ability is, in brief, the ability to use and understand words. Vocabulary and grammar tests are typical measures of this ability. Reading comprehension or paragraph interpretation questions are common in many kinds of civil service tests. You are given a paragraph of written material and asked to find its central meaning.

3) Numerical ability

Number skills can be tested by the familiar arithmetic problem, by checking paired lists of numbers to see which are alike and which are different, or by interpreting charts and graphs. In the latter test, a graph may be printed in the test booklet which you are asked to use as the basis for answering questions.

4) Observation

A popular test for law-enforcement positions is the observation test. A picture is shown to you for several minutes, then taken away. Questions about the picture test your ability to observe both details and larger elements.

5) Following directions

In many positions in the public service, the employee must be able to carry out written instructions dependably and accurately. You may be given a chart with several columns, each column listing a variety of information. The questions require you to carry out directions involving the information given in the chart.

6) Skills and aptitudes

Performance tests effectively measure some manual skills and aptitudes. When the skill is one in which you are trained, such as typing or shorthand, you can practice. These tests are often very much like those given in business school or high school courses. For many of the other skills and aptitudes, however, no short-time preparation can be made. Skills and abilities natural to you or that you have developed throughout your lifetime are being tested.

Many of the general questions just described provide all the data needed to answer the questions and ask you to use your reasoning ability to find the answers. Your best preparation for these tests, as well as for tests of facts and ideas, is to be at your physical and mental best. You, no doubt, have your own methods of getting into an exam-taking mood and keeping "in shape." The next section lists some ideas on this subject.

IV. KINDS OF QUESTIONS

Only rarely is the "essay" question, which you answer in narrative form, used in civil service tests. Civil service tests are usually of the short-answer type. Full instructions for answering these questions will be given to you at the examination. But in case this is your first experience with short-answer questions and separate answer sheets, here is what you need to know:

1) **Multiple-choice Questions**

Most popular of the short-answer questions is the "multiple choice" or "best answer" question. It can be used, for example, to test for factual knowledge, ability to solve problems or judgment in meeting situations found at work.

A multiple-choice question is normally one of three types—
- It can begin with an incomplete statement followed by several possible endings. You are to find the one ending which *best* completes the statement, although some of the others may not be entirely wrong.
- It can also be a complete statement in the form of a question which is answered by choosing one of the statements listed.

- It can be in the form of a problem – again you select the best answer.

Here is an example of a multiple-choice question with a discussion which should give you some clues as to the method for choosing the right answer:

When an employee has a complaint about his assignment, the action which will *best* help him overcome his difficulty is to
- A. discuss his difficulty with his coworkers
- B. take the problem to the head of the organization
- C. take the problem to the person who gave him the assignment
- D. say nothing to anyone about his complaint

In answering this question, you should study each of the choices to find which is best. Consider choice "A" – Certainly an employee may discuss his complaint with fellow employees, but no change or improvement can result, and the complaint remains unresolved. Choice "B" is a poor choice since the head of the organization probably does not know what assignment you have been given, and taking your problem to him is known as "going over the head" of the supervisor. The supervisor, or person who made the assignment, is the person who can clarify it or correct any injustice. Choice "C" is, therefore, correct. To say nothing, as in choice "D," is unwise. Supervisors have and interest in knowing the problems employees are facing, and the employee is seeking a solution to his problem.

2) True/False Questions

The "true/false" or "right/wrong" form of question is sometimes used. Here a complete statement is given. Your job is to decide whether the statement is right or wrong.

SAMPLE: A roaming cell-phone call to a nearby city costs less than a non-roaming call to a distant city.

This statement is wrong, or false, since roaming calls are more expensive.

This is not a complete list of all possible question forms, although most of the others are variations of these common types. You will always get complete directions for answering questions. Be sure you understand *how* to mark your answers – ask questions until you do.

V. RECORDING YOUR ANSWERS

Computer terminals are used more and more today for many different kinds of exams.
For an examination with very few applicants, you may be told to record your answers in the test booklet itself. Separate answer sheets are much more common. If this separate answer sheet is to be scored by machine – and this is often the case – it is highly important that you mark your answers correctly in order to get credit.
An electronic scoring machine is often used in civil service offices because of the speed with which papers can be scored. Machine-scored answer sheets must be marked with a pencil, which will be given to you. This pencil has a high graphite content which responds to the electronic scoring machine. As a matter of fact, stray dots may register as answers, so do not let your pencil rest on the answer sheet while you are pondering the correct answer. Also, if your pencil lead breaks or is otherwise defective, ask for another.

Since the answer sheet will be dropped in a slot in the scoring machine, be careful not to bend the corners or get the paper crumpled.

The answer sheet normally has five vertical columns of numbers, with 30 numbers to a column. These numbers correspond to the question numbers in your test booklet. After each number, going across the page are four or five pairs of dotted lines. These short dotted lines have small letters or numbers above them. The first two pairs may also have a "T" or "F" above the letters. This indicates that the first two pairs only are to be used if the questions are of the true-false type. If the questions are multiple choice, disregard the "T" and "F" and pay attention only to the small letters or numbers.

Answer your questions in the manner of the sample that follows:

32. The largest city in the United States is
    A. Washington, D.C.
    B. New York City
    C. Chicago
    D. Detroit
    E. San Francisco

1) Choose the answer you think is best. (New York City is the largest, so "B" is correct.)
2) Find the row of dotted lines numbered the same as the question you are answering. (Find row number 32)
3) Find the pair of dotted lines corresponding to the answer. (Find the pair of lines under the mark "B.")
4) Make a solid black mark between the dotted lines.

VI. BEFORE THE TEST

Common sense will help you find procedures to follow to get ready for an examination. Too many of us, however, overlook these sensible measures. Indeed, nervousness and fatigue have been found to be the most serious reasons why applicants fail to do their best on civil service tests. Here is a list of reminders:

- Begin your preparation early – Don't wait until the last minute to go scurrying around for books and materials or to find out what the position is all about.
- Prepare continuously – An hour a night for a week is better than an all-night cram session. This has been definitely established. What is more, a night a week for a month will return better dividends than crowding your study into a shorter period of time.
- Locate the place of the exam – You have been sent a notice telling you when and where to report for the examination. If the location is in a different town or otherwise unfamiliar to you, it would be well to inquire the best route and learn something about the building.
- Relax the night before the test – Allow your mind to rest. Do not study at all that night. Plan some mild recreation or diversion; then go to bed early and get a good night's sleep.
- Get up early enough to make a leisurely trip to the place for the test – This way unforeseen events, traffic snarls, unfamiliar buildings, etc. will not upset you.
- Dress comfortably – A written test is not a fashion show. You will be known by number and not by name, so wear something comfortable.

- Leave excess paraphernalia at home – Shopping bags and odd bundles will get in your way. You need bring only the items mentioned in the official notice you received; usually everything you need is provided. Do not bring reference books to the exam. They will only confuse those last minutes and be taken away from you when in the test room.
- Arrive somewhat ahead of time – If because of transportation schedules you must get there very early, bring a newspaper or magazine to take your mind off yourself while waiting.
- Locate the examination room – When you have found the proper room, you will be directed to the seat or part of the room where you will sit. Sometimes you are given a sheet of instructions to read while you are waiting. Do not fill out any forms until you are told to do so; just read them and be prepared.
- Relax and prepare to listen to the instructions
- If you have any physical problem that may keep you from doing your best, be sure to tell the test administrator. If you are sick or in poor health, you really cannot do your best on the exam. You can come back and take the test some other time.

VII. AT THE TEST

The day of the test is here and you have the test booklet in your hand. The temptation to get going is very strong. Caution! There is more to success than knowing the right answers. You must know how to identify your papers and understand variations in the type of short-answer question used in this particular examination. Follow these suggestions for maximum results from your efforts:

1) Cooperate with the monitor

The test administrator has a duty to create a situation in which you can be as much at ease as possible. He will give instructions, tell you when to begin, check to see that you are marking your answer sheet correctly, and so on. He is not there to guard you, although he will see that your competitors do not take unfair advantage. He wants to help you do your best.

2) Listen to all instructions

Don't jump the gun! Wait until you understand all directions. In most civil service tests you get more time than you need to answer the questions. So don't be in a hurry. Read each word of instructions until you clearly understand the meaning. Study the examples, listen to all announcements and follow directions. Ask questions if you do not understand what to do.

3) Identify your papers

Civil service exams are usually identified by number only. You will be assigned a number; you must not put your name on your test papers. Be sure to copy your number correctly. Since more than one exam may be given, copy your exact examination title.

4) Plan your time

Unless you are told that a test is a "speed" or "rate of work" test, speed itself is usually not important. Time enough to answer all the questions will be provided, but this does not mean that you have all day. An overall time limit has been set. Divide the total time (in minutes) by the number of questions to determine the approximate time you have for each question.

5) Do not linger over difficult questions

If you come across a difficult question, mark it with a paper clip (useful to have along) and come back to it when you have been through the booklet. One caution if you do this – be sure to skip a number on your answer sheet as well. Check often to be sure that you have not lost your place and that you are marking in the row numbered the same as the question you are answering.

6) Read the questions

Be sure you know what the question asks! Many capable people are unsuccessful because they failed to *read* the questions correctly.

7) Answer all questions

Unless you have been instructed that a penalty will be deducted for incorrect answers, it is better to guess than to omit a question.

8) Speed tests

It is often better NOT to guess on speed tests. It has been found that on timed tests people are tempted to spend the last few seconds before time is called in marking answers at random – without even reading them – in the hope of picking up a few extra points. To discourage this practice, the instructions may warn you that your score will be "corrected" for guessing. That is, a penalty will be applied. The incorrect answers will be deducted from the correct ones, or some other penalty formula will be used.

9) Review your answers

If you finish before time is called, go back to the questions you guessed or omitted to give them further thought. Review other answers if you have time.

10) Return your test materials

If you are ready to leave before others have finished or time is called, take ALL your materials to the monitor and leave quietly. Never take any test material with you. The monitor can discover whose papers are not complete, and taking a test booklet may be grounds for disqualification.

VIII. EXAMINATION TECHNIQUES

1) Read the general instructions carefully. These are usually printed on the first page of the exam booklet. As a rule, these instructions refer to the timing of the examination; the fact that you should not start work until the signal and must stop work at a signal, etc. If there are any *special* instructions, such as a choice of questions to be answered, make sure that you note this instruction carefully.

2) When you are ready to start work on the examination, that is as soon as the signal has been given, read the instructions to each question booklet, underline any key words or phrases, such as *least, best, outline, describe* and the like. In this way you will tend to answer as requested rather than discover on reviewing your paper that you *listed without describing*, that you selected the *worst* choice rather than the *best* choice, etc.

3) If the examination is of the objective or multiple-choice type – that is, each question will also give a series of possible answers: A, B, C or D, and you are called upon to select the best answer and write the letter next to that answer on your answer paper – it is advisable to start answering each question in turn. There may be anywhere from 50 to 100 such questions in the three or four hours allotted and you can see how much time would be taken if you read through all the questions before beginning to answer any. Furthermore, if you come across a question or group of questions which you know would be difficult to answer, it would undoubtedly affect your handling of all the other questions.

4) If the examination is of the essay type and contains but a few questions, it is a moot point as to whether you should read all the questions before starting to answer any one. Of course, if you are given a choice – say five out of seven and the like – then it is essential to read all the questions so you can eliminate the two that are most difficult. If, however, you are asked to answer all the questions, there may be danger in trying to answer the easiest one first because you may find that you will spend too much time on it. The best technique is to answer the first question, then proceed to the second, etc.

5) Time your answers. Before the exam begins, write down the time it started, then add the time allowed for the examination and write down the time it must be completed, then divide the time available somewhat as follows:
    - If 3-1/2 hours are allowed, that would be 210 minutes. If you have 80 objective-type questions, that would be an average of 2-1/2 minutes per question. Allow yourself no more than 2 minutes per question, or a total of 160 minutes, which will permit about 50 minutes to review.
    - If for the time allotment of 210 minutes there are 7 essay questions to answer, that would average about 30 minutes a question. Give yourself only 25 minutes per question so that you have about 35 minutes to review.

6) The most important instruction is to *read each question* and make sure you know what is wanted. The second most important instruction is to *time yourself properly* so that you answer every question. The third most important instruction is to *answer every question*. Guess if you have to but include something for each question. Remember that you will receive no credit for a blank and will probably receive some credit if you write something in answer to an essay question. If you guess a letter – say "B" for a multiple-choice question – you may have guessed right. If you leave a blank as an answer to a multiple-choice question, the examiners may respect your feelings but it will not add a point to your score. Some exams may penalize you for wrong answers, so in such cases *only*, you may not want to guess unless you have some basis for your answer.

7) Suggestions
    a. Objective-type questions
        1. Examine the question booklet for proper sequence of pages and questions
        2. Read all instructions carefully
        3. Skip any question which seems too difficult; return to it after all other questions have been answered
        4. Apportion your time properly; do not spend too much time on any single question or group of questions

5. Note and underline key words – *all, most, fewest, least, best, worst, same, opposite*, etc.
6. Pay particular attention to negatives
7. Note unusual option, e.g., unduly long, short, complex, different or similar in content to the body of the question
8. Observe the use of "hedging" words – *probably, may, most likely,* etc.
9. Make sure that your answer is put next to the same number as the question
10. Do not second-guess unless you have good reason to believe the second answer is definitely more correct
11. Cross out original answer if you decide another answer is more accurate; do not erase until you are ready to hand your paper in
12. Answer all questions; guess unless instructed otherwise
13. Leave time for review

b. Essay questions
1. Read each question carefully
2. Determine exactly what is wanted. Underline key words or phrases.
3. Decide on outline or paragraph answer
4. Include many different points and elements unless asked to develop any one or two points or elements
5. Show impartiality by giving pros and cons unless directed to select one side only
6. Make and write down any assumptions you find necessary to answer the questions
7. Watch your English, grammar, punctuation and choice of words
8. Time your answers; don't crowd material

8) Answering the essay question

Most essay questions can be answered by framing the specific response around several key words or ideas. Here are a few such key words or ideas:

M's: manpower, materials, methods, money, management
P's: purpose, program, policy, plan, procedure, practice, problems, pitfalls, personnel, public relations

a. Six basic steps in handling problems:
1. Preliminary plan and background development
2. Collect information, data and facts
3. Analyze and interpret information, data and facts
4. Analyze and develop solutions as well as make recommendations
5. Prepare report and sell recommendations
6. Install recommendations and follow up effectiveness

b. Pitfalls to avoid
1. *Taking things for granted* – A statement of the situation does not necessarily imply that each of the elements is necessarily true; for example, a complaint may be invalid and biased so that all that can be taken for granted is that a complaint has been registered

2. *Considering only one side of a situation* – Wherever possible, indicate several alternatives and then point out the reasons you selected the best one
3. *Failing to indicate follow up* – Whenever your answer indicates action on your part, make certain that you will take proper follow-up action to see how successful your recommendations, procedures or actions turn out to be
4. *Taking too long in answering any single question* – Remember to time your answers properly

IX. AFTER THE TEST

Scoring procedures differ in detail among civil service jurisdictions although the general principles are the same. Whether the papers are hand-scored or graded by machine we have described, they are nearly always graded by number. That is, the person who marks the paper knows only the number – never the name – of the applicant. Not until all the papers have been graded will they be matched with names. If other tests, such as training and experience or oral interview ratings have been given, scores will be combined. Different parts of the examination usually have different weights. For example, the written test might count 60 percent of the final grade, and a rating of training and experience 40 percent. In many jurisdictions, veterans will have a certain number of points added to their grades.

After the final grade has been determined, the names are placed in grade order and an eligible list is established. There are various methods for resolving ties between those who get the same final grade – probably the most common is to place first the name of the person whose application was received first. Job offers are made from the eligible list in the order the names appear on it. You will be notified of your grade and your rank as soon as all these computations have been made. This will be done as rapidly as possible.

People who are found to meet the requirements in the announcement are called "eligibles." Their names are put on a list of eligible candidates. An eligible's chances of getting a job depend on how high he stands on this list and how fast agencies are filling jobs from the list.

When a job is to be filled from a list of eligibles, the agency asks for the names of people on the list of eligibles for that job. When the civil service commission receives this request, it sends to the agency the names of the three people highest on this list. Or, if the job to be filled has specialized requirements, the office sends the agency the names of the top three persons who meet these requirements from the general list.

The appointing officer makes a choice from among the three people whose names were sent to him. If the selected person accepts the appointment, the names of the others are put back on the list to be considered for future openings.

That is the rule in hiring from all kinds of eligible lists, whether they are for typist, carpenter, chemist, or something else. For every vacancy, the appointing officer has his choice of any one of the top three eligibles on the list. This explains why the person whose name is on top of the list sometimes does not get an appointment when some of the persons lower on the list do. If the appointing officer chooses the second or third eligible, the No. 1 eligible does not get a job at once, but stays on the list until he is appointed or the list is terminated.

X. HOW TO PASS THE INTERVIEW TEST

The examination for which you applied requires an oral interview test. You have already taken the written test and you are now being called for the interview test – the final part of the formal examination.

You may think that it is not possible to prepare for an interview test and that there are no procedures to follow during an interview. Our purpose is to point out some things you can do in advance that will help you and some good rules to follow and pitfalls to avoid while you are being interviewed.

What is an interview supposed to test?

The written examination is designed to test the technical knowledge and competence of the candidate; the oral is designed to evaluate intangible qualities, not readily measured otherwise, and to establish a list showing the relative fitness of each candidate – as measured against his competitors – for the position sought. Scoring is not on the basis of "right" and "wrong," but on a sliding scale of values ranging from "not passable" to "outstanding." As a matter of fact, it is possible to achieve a relatively low score without a single "incorrect" answer because of evident weakness in the qualities being measured.

Occasionally, an examination may consist entirely of an oral test – either an individual or a group oral. In such cases, information is sought concerning the technical knowledges and abilities of the candidate, since there has been no written examination for this purpose. More commonly, however, an oral test is used to supplement a written examination.

Who conducts interviews?

The composition of oral boards varies among different jurisdictions. In nearly all, a representative of the personnel department serves as chairman. One of the members of the board may be a representative of the department in which the candidate would work. In some cases, "outside experts" are used, and, frequently, a businessman or some other representative of the general public is asked to serve. Labor and management or other special groups may be represented. The aim is to secure the services of experts in the appropriate field.

However the board is composed, it is a good idea (and not at all improper or unethical) to ascertain in advance of the interview who the members are and what groups they represent. When you are introduced to them, you will have some idea of their backgrounds and interests, and at least you will not stutter and stammer over their names.

What should be done before the interview?

While knowledge about the board members is useful and takes some of the surprise element out of the interview, there is other preparation which is more substantive. It *is* possible to prepare for an oral interview – in several ways:

1) Keep a copy of your application and review it carefully before the interview

This may be the only document before the oral board, and the starting point of the interview. Know what education and experience you have listed there, and the sequence and dates of all of it. Sometimes the board will ask you to review the highlights of your experience for them; you should not have to hem and haw doing it.

2) Study the class specification and the examination announcement

Usually, the oral board has one or both of these to guide them. The qualities, characteristics or knowledges required by the position sought are stated in these documents. They offer valuable clues as to the nature of the oral interview. For example, if the job involves supervisory responsibilities, the announcement will usually indicate that knowledge of modern supervisory methods and the qualifications of the candidate as a supervisor will be tested. If so, you can expect such questions, frequently in the form of a hypothetical situation which you are expected to solve. NEVER go into an oral without knowledge of the duties and responsibilities of the job you seek.

3) Think through each qualification required

Try to visualize the kind of questions you would ask if you were a board member. How well could you answer them? Try especially to appraise your own knowledge and background in each area, *measured against the job sought*, and identify any areas in which you are weak. Be critical and realistic – do not flatter yourself.

4) Do some general reading in areas in which you feel you may be weak

For example, if the job involves supervision and your past experience has NOT, some general reading in supervisory methods and practices, particularly in the field of human relations, might be useful. Do NOT study agency procedures or detailed manuals. The oral board will be testing your understanding and capacity, not your memory.

5) Get a good night's sleep and watch your general health and mental attitude

You will want a clear head at the interview. Take care of a cold or any other minor ailment, and of course, no hangovers.

What should be done on the day of the interview?

Now comes the day of the interview itself. Give yourself plenty of time to get there. Plan to arrive somewhat ahead of the scheduled time, particularly if your appointment is in the fore part of the day. If a previous candidate fails to appear, the board might be ready for you a bit early. By early afternoon an oral board is almost invariably behind schedule if there are many candidates, and you may have to wait. Take along a book or magazine to read, or your application to review, but leave any extraneous material in the waiting room when you go in for your interview. In any event, relax and compose yourself.

The matter of dress is important. The board is forming impressions about you – from your experience, your manners, your attitude, and your appearance. Give your personal appearance careful attention. Dress your best, but not your flashiest. Choose conservative, appropriate clothing, and be sure it is immaculate. This is a business interview, and your appearance should indicate that you regard it as such. Besides, being well groomed and properly dressed will help boost your confidence.

Sooner or later, someone will call your name and escort you into the interview room. *This is it.* From here on you are on your own. It is too late for any more preparation. But remember, you asked for this opportunity to prove your fitness, and you are here because your request was granted.

What happens when you go in?

The usual sequence of events will be as follows: The clerk (who is often the board stenographer) will introduce you to the chairman of the oral board, who will introduce you to the other members of the board. Acknowledge the introductions before you sit down. Do not be surprised if you find a microphone facing you or a stenotypist sitting by. Oral interviews are usually recorded in the event of an appeal or other review.

Usually the chairman of the board will open the interview by reviewing the highlights of your education and work experience from your application – primarily for the benefit of the other members of the board, as well as to get the material into the record. Do not interrupt or comment unless there is an error or significant misinterpretation; if that is the case, do not hesitate. But do not quibble about insignificant matters. Also, he will usually ask you some question about your education, experience or your present job – partly to get you to start talking and to establish the interviewing "rapport." He may start the actual questioning, or turn it over to one of the other members. Frequently, each member undertakes the questioning on a particular area, one in which he is perhaps most competent, so you can expect each member to participate in the examination. Because time is limited, you may also expect some rather abrupt switches in the direction the questioning takes, so do not be upset by it. Normally, a board member will not pursue a single line of questioning unless he discovers a particular strength or weakness.

After each member has participated, the chairman will usually ask whether any member has any further questions, then will ask you if you have anything you wish to add. Unless you are expecting this question, it may floor you. Worse, it may start you off on an extended, extemporaneous speech. The board is not usually seeking more information. The question is principally to offer you a last opportunity to present further qualifications or to indicate that you have nothing to add. So, if you feel that a significant qualification or characteristic has been overlooked, it is proper to point it out in a sentence or so. Do not compliment the board on the thoroughness of their examination – they have been sketchy, and you know it. If you wish, merely say, "No thank you, I have nothing further to add." This is a point where you can "talk yourself out" of a good impression or fail to present an important bit of information. Remember, *you close the interview yourself*.

The chairman will then say, "That is all, Mr. _____, thank you." Do not be startled; the interview is over, and quicker than you think. Thank him, gather your belongings and take your leave. Save your sigh of relief for the other side of the door.

How to put your best foot forward

Throughout this entire process, you may feel that the board individually and collectively is trying to pierce your defenses, seek out your hidden weaknesses and embarrass and confuse you. Actually, this is not true. They are obliged to make an appraisal of your qualifications for the job you are seeking, and they want to see you in your best light. Remember, they must interview all candidates and a non-cooperative candidate may become a failure in spite of their best efforts to bring out his qualifications. Here are 15 suggestions that will help you:

1) Be natural – Keep your attitude confident, not cocky

If you are not confident that you can do the job, do not expect the board to be. Do not apologize for your weaknesses, try to bring out your strong points. The board is interested in a positive, not negative, presentation. Cockiness will antagonize any board member and make him wonder if you are covering up a weakness by a false show of strength.

2) Get comfortable, but don't lounge or sprawl

Sit erectly but not stiffly. A careless posture may lead the board to conclude that you are careless in other things, or at least that you are not impressed by the importance of the occasion. Either conclusion is natural, even if incorrect. Do not fuss with your clothing, a pencil or an ashtray. Your hands may occasionally be useful to emphasize a point; do not let them become a point of distraction.

3) Do not wisecrack or make small talk

This is a serious situation, and your attitude should show that you consider it as such. Further, the time of the board is limited – they do not want to waste it, and neither should you.

4) Do not exaggerate your experience or abilities

In the first place, from information in the application or other interviews and sources, the board may know more about you than you think. Secondly, you probably will not get away with it. An experienced board is rather adept at spotting such a situation, so do not take the chance.

5) If you know a board member, do not make a point of it, yet do not hide it

Certainly you are not fooling him, and probably not the other members of the board. Do not try to take advantage of your acquaintanceship – it will probably do you little good.

6) Do not dominate the interview

Let the board do that. They will give you the clues – do not assume that you have to do all the talking. Realize that the board has a number of questions to ask you, and do not try to take up all the interview time by showing off your extensive knowledge of the answer to the first one.

7) Be attentive

You only have 20 minutes or so, and you should keep your attention at its sharpest throughout. When a member is addressing a problem or question to you, give him your undivided attention. Address your reply principally to him, but do not exclude the other board members.

8) Do not interrupt

A board member may be stating a problem for you to analyze. He will ask you a question when the time comes. Let him state the problem, and wait for the question.

9) Make sure you understand the question

Do not try to answer until you are sure what the question is. If it is not clear, restate it in your own words or ask the board member to clarify it for you. However, do not haggle about minor elements.

10) Reply promptly but not hastily

A common entry on oral board rating sheets is "candidate responded readily," or "candidate hesitated in replies." Respond as promptly and quickly as you can, but do not jump to a hasty, ill-considered answer.

11) Do not be peremptory in your answers

A brief answer is proper – but do not fire your answer back. That is a losing game from your point of view. The board member can probably ask questions much faster than you can answer them.

12) Do not try to create the answer you think the board member wants

He is interested in what kind of mind you have and how it works – not in playing games. Furthermore, he can usually spot this practice and will actually grade you down on it.

13) Do not switch sides in your reply merely to agree with a board member

Frequently, a member will take a contrary position merely to draw you out and to see if you are willing and able to defend your point of view. Do not start a debate, yet do not surrender a good position. If a position is worth taking, it is worth defending.

14) Do not be afraid to admit an error in judgment if you are shown to be wrong

The board knows that you are forced to reply without any opportunity for careful consideration. Your answer may be demonstrably wrong. If so, admit it and get on with the interview.

15) Do not dwell at length on your present job

The opening question may relate to your present assignment. Answer the question but do not go into an extended discussion. You are being examined for a *new* job, not your present one. As a matter of fact, try to phrase ALL your answers in terms of the job for which you are being examined.

Basis of Rating

Probably you will forget most of these "do's" and "don'ts" when you walk into the oral interview room. Even remembering them all will not ensure you a passing grade. Perhaps you did not have the qualifications in the first place. But remembering them will help you to put your best foot forward, without treading on the toes of the board members.

Rumor and popular opinion to the contrary notwithstanding, an oral board wants you to make the best appearance possible. They know you are under pressure – but they also want to see how you respond to it as a guide to what your reaction would be under the pressures of the job you seek. They will be influenced by the degree of poise you display, the personal traits you show and the manner in which you respond.

ABOUT THIS BOOK

This book contains tests divided into Examination Sections. Go through each test, answering every question in the margin. We have also attached a sample answer sheet at the back of the book that can be removed and used. At the end of each test look at the answer key and check your answers. On the ones you got wrong, look at the right answer choice and learn. Do not fill in the answers first. Do not memorize the questions and answers, but understand the answer and principles involved. On your test, the questions will likely be different from the samples. Questions are changed and new ones added. If you understand these past questions you should have success with any changes that arise. Tests may consist of several types of questions. We have additional books on each subject should more study be advisable or necessary for you. Finally, the more you study, the better prepared you will be. This book is intended to be the last thing you study before you walk into the examination room. Prior study of relevant texts is also recommended. NLC publishes some of these in our Fundamental Series. Knowledge and good sense are important factors in passing your exam. Good luck also helps. So now study this Passbook, absorb the material contained within and take that knowledge into the examination. Then do your best to pass that exam.

EXAMINATION SECTION

EXAMINATION SECTION
TEST 1

DIRECTIONS: Each question or incomplete statement is followed by several suggested answers or completions. Select the one that BEST answers the question or completes the statement. *PRINT THE LETTER OF THE CORRECT ANSWER IN THE SPACE AT THE RIGHT.*

Questions 1-3.

DIRECTIONS: Questions 1 through 3 are to be answered on the basis of the following schedule for running time. Running time is the scheduled time for a bus to travel from one stop to the next. The arrow indicates the direction in which the bus travels. For example, the running time from Main St. to School St., eastbound, is 5 minutes during the hours from 10:00 P.M. to 6:00 A.M. and 9 minutes from 6:00 A.M. to 10:00 P.M. If you want to know when a bus that leaves School St. at 11:00 P.M. should arrive at Pearl St., you should add the 14 minutes running time to 11:00 P.M. to obtain 11:14 P.M.

RUNNING TIME

Bus Stop	10:00 PM to 6:00 AM		6:00 AM to 10:00 PM	
	Eastbound	Westbound	Eastbound	Westbound
Main St to School St.	5	6	9	11
to Bank St.	4	5	7	28
to Market St.	5	6	10	12
to Pearl St.	5	6	9	11
to State St.	4	5	7	8
Totals	23	28	42	50

1. An eastbound bus leaves School St. at 1:30 P.M. At what time will it arrive at Market St.?
   A. 1:39   B. 1:41   C. 1:47   D. 1:50   1.____

2. If a passenger boarding a westbound bus at State St. wishes to be at Bank St. by 3:00 P.M., he last bus he should take is one that leaves no later than _____ P.M.
   A. 2:21   B. 2:29   C. 2:34   D. 2:43   2.____

3. A westbound bus leaves Pearl St. at 11 P.M. but has an 18 minute delay because off a sick passenger at Market St. The bus is delayed for another 4 minutes due to a broken traffic light at School St.
   What time will the bus arrive at Main St.?
   A. 11:45 P.M.   B. 11:50 P.M.   C. 12:07 A.M.   D. 12:15 A.M.   3.____

4. To help prevent passenger accidents inside a bus, which of the following starting and stopping procedures should a bus operator follow? _____ acceleration when starting and _____ when stopping.
   A. Gradual; gradual slowing down
   B. Rapid; rapid braking
   C. Gradual; rapid braking
   D. Rapid; gradual slowing down

5. When a bus operator is driving a bus, a flashing yellow light at an intersection means that he should
   A. stop
   B. stop, then proceed slowly
   C. proceed with caution
   D. maintain his speed through the intersection

Questions 6-8.

DIRECTIONS: Questions 6 through 8 are to be answered on the basis of the following schedule for Headway. Headway is the scheduled time between one bus and the next bus, and this varies according to the time of day. For example, from 12 Noon to 4:00 P.M., the time between buses is 10 minutes, and from 5:00 A.M. to 9:00 A.M. it is 5 minutes.

HEADWAY

			Minutes
5:00 A.M.	to	9:00 A.M.	5
9:00 A.M.	to	12:00 Noon	8
12:00 Noon	to	4:00 P.M.	10
4:00 P.M.	to	7:00 P.M.	5
7:00 P.M.	to	11:00 P.M.	15
11:00 P.M.	to	5:00 A.M.	30

6. At 7:00 A.M., a man just misses a bus.
   About how many minutes will he have to wait for the next bus?
   A. 5   B. 8   C. 9   D. 11

7. At 8:33 P.M., a woman arrives at a bus stop. The last bus left her stop on schedule 3 minutes ago. The next scheduled bus has been cancelled due to faulty equipment. The bus following the cancelled bus is running three minutes late because of heavy traffic.
   At what time should another bus arrive at the woman's stop?
   A. 8:40 A.M.   B. 8:57 P.M.   C. 9:03 P.M.   D. 9:06 P.M.

8. What is the difference between the headway times at 11:50 A.M. and 11:20 P.M.?
   A. 15   B. 20   C. 22   D. 25

9. In heavy traffic, which of the following turn situations is potentially MOST hazardous? 9._____
   A. Right turn from one two-way street onto another two-way street
   B. Left turn from a one-way street onto a two-way street
   C. Right turn from a two-way street onto a one-way street
   D. Left turn from one two-way street onto another two-way street

10. As you approach an intersection in your bus, you note that the traffic light is red and you hear the wailing noise of an ambulance siren. A police officer at the intersection motions for you to go through the light. 10._____
    Under the circumstances, you should
    A. stop until you can determine the location of the ambulance
    B. stop until the light turns green, then proceed
    C. proceed to the middle of the intersection and stop so that you can better determine the location of the ambulance
    D. proceed through the intersection

11. Which of the following actions should a bus operator take if he notices a boy climbing on the back of his bus? 11._____
    A. Reduce speed and continue on his route
    B. Make sudden stops and starts to shake the boy off
    C. Stop the bus, inform his passengers why he is stopping, and then order the boy off the bus
    D. Ignore the boy and continue his trip at a normal speed

Questions 12-15.

DIRECTIONS: Questions 12 through 15 are to be answered on the basis of the following schedule. Running time is the scheduled time for a bus to travel from one stop to the next. The arrow indicates the direction in which the bus travels. For example, the running time from the Railroad Station to Main & Oak is 5 minutes. Layover time is the time spent at the terminal before leaving on the next trip.

Bus Stop	Southbound Running Time (Minutes)	Northbound Running Time (Minutes)
Railroad Station	(leaves	5
Main & Oak	5	4
Main & Elm	4	6
Main & Ash	6	3
Main & Pine	3	5
Main & Birch	5	4
Farmer's Market	4	8
Plum & State	8	7
Apple & State	7	7
Pear & State	7	6
Peach & State	6	5
Court House	5	(Leaves

Note: Layover time at each of the terminals, Railroad Station Terminal and Court House, is 5 minutes.

12. What is the running time, in minutes, from Peach & State northbound to Main & Ash?
    A. 37 B. 40 C. 42 D. 45

13. If a bus leaves the Railroad Station at 8:10 A.M., at what time should it arrive at the Court House? _____ A.M.
    A. 9:05 B. 9:08 C. 9:10 D. 9:12

14. If a bus leaves the Court House at 9:05 A.M., at what time should it arrive at Farmer's Market? _____ A.M.
    A. 9:30 B. 9:35 C. 9:38 D. 9:43

15. How much time will it take a bus leaving Main & Pine southbound to arrive back at Main & Pine on the return trip? 1 hour, _____ minutes.
    A. 17 B. 19 C. 29 D. 33

Questions 16-20.

DIRECTIONS: Questions 16 through 20 are to be answered SOLELY on the basis of the Bus Operator's Daily Trip Sheet shown below. At each terminal, at the end of a trip, the operator takes the readings on the cash counter and fare card counter which are a part of the fare box and enters them on the Bus Operator's Daily Trip Sheet. The part of the Bus Operator's Daily Trip Sheet shown below is a record of the fare box readings for a specific working day for Bus Operator Birch. Note that a trip covers the distance from one terminal to the other. When Operator Birch left the Rowland Street Terminal for the first trip of his working day, the cash counter registered $677.25 from a previous operator's run, and the fare card counter registered 113 fares. Birch left Rowland Terminal at 12:51 P.M. and completed his first trip over the route and arrived at the Tully Street Terminal at 1:28 P.M. Assume that at each terminal arriving and leaving times are identical. For the remainder of his working day, he rode back and forth along his route, arriving at the Rowland and Tully Terminals at the times indicated on the Bus Operator's Daily Trip Sheet. His fare box readings were taken and entered on the trip sheet shown below immediately upon arrival at the terminals. When answering these questions, assume the fare is $2.25 and that all passengers are required to pay the full fare. Also assume that the card fares collected are worth $2.25 each.

BUS OPERATOR'S DAILY TRIP SHEET

Point Leaving From	Time	Fare Box Readings at the End of Each Trip	
		Cash	Cards
Rowland Street Terminal	12:51 PM	677.25	113
Tully Street Terminal	1:28 PM	756.00	117
Rowland Street Terminal	2:08 PM	810.00	122
Tully Street Terminal	2:45 PM	893.25	131
Rowland Street Terminal	3:25 PM	987.75	133
Tully Street Terminal	4:04 PM	1,102.50	144
Rowland Street Terminal	3:38 PM	1,212.75	147
Tully Street Terminal	5:18 PM	1,233.00	148

16. How much cash was collected between 1:28 P.M. and 3:25 P.M.? 16._____
    A. $198.75   B. $228.75   C. $231.75   D. $326.25

17. How many fares were collected between 2:45 P.M. and 4:38 P.M.? 17._____
    A. 16   B. 17   C. 25   D. 147

18. What is the value of the card fares collected from 12:51 P.M. to 5:18 P.M.? 18._____
    A. $74.25   B. $78.75   C. $81.00   D. $83.25

19. How many passengers got on the bus between 2:08 P.M. and 4:04 P.M.? 19._____
    A. 144   B. 152   C. 157   D. 176

20. What was the total number of passengers carried during the entire run from 12:51 P.M. to 5:18 P.M.? 20._____
    A. 245   B. 269   C. 282   D. 583

Questions 21-27.

DIRECTIONS: Questions 21 through 27 are to be answered SOLELY on the basis of the description of the accident and the Accident Report shown below and on the following page. The Accident Report contains 38 numbered spaces. Read the description and look at the Accident Report before answering these questions.

Description of Accident: At 1:15 P.M. on July 20, 2020, an auto with license plate #51VOMNY, driven by Martha Ryan, license number R21692-33739-295897-41, and owned by George Ryan, leaving east on Fulton Street, crashed into the right front wheel of a moving Flxible bus, T.A. Vehicle No. 7026, license plate no. 10346-K, at the intersection of Jay Street and Fulton Street. The bus was covering Run 12 on Route B67. The auto was a green 2013 Chevrolet Malibu. The bus with 15 passengers was traveling south on Jay Street. The bus had a green traffic light in its favor at the Jay St.-Fulton St. intersection. The bus driver was Art Simmons, Badge No. 5712, license number S24368-35274-263745-42.

Two passengers in the bus fell onto the floor. An elderly woman (age 65) bruised her left knee. A male (age 25) bruised the palm of his right hand. The auto driver's daughter, Mary (age 19), who was in the right front seat, bumped her head on the windshield. The police and an ambulance were summoned. The three injured persons were taken to Cumberland Hospital by Attendant John Hawkins. Police Officer Thomas Brown, Badge No. 2354, from the 68th Precinct, took statements from witnesses to the accident.

ACCIDENT REPORT
TO BE FILLED IN BY BUS OPERATOR

Route _1_ Run _2_ T.A. Vehicle Type: Bus Truck Auto Other Vehicle _3_ T.A. Vehicle No. _4_ T.A. License Plate No. _5_ Make _6_ Date of Accident _7_ Hour _8_ Street Lights On _9_
Place of Accident _____10_____
Direction of T.A. Vehicle _11_ Direction of Other Vehicle _12_
State if operating on one- or two-way street: T.A. Vehicle _13_ way Other vehicle: _14_ way
Did accident occur in bus stop area? _____15_____
Number of passengers in T.A. Vehicle _16_
Number of persons in other vehicle _17_
Traffic lights involved _18_ Color of same when leaving near corner _19_ Was ambulance called? _20_ Persons taken to what hospital? _21_
Was police officer present? _22_ Officer's No. _23_ Precinct _24_
Name of owner of other vehicle _25_
License No. of other vehicle _26_
Address of owner of other vehicle _____27_____
Color of other vehicle _28_ Model of other vehicle _29_
Year of other vehicle _30_ Make of other vehicle _31_
Name of driver of other vehicle _____32_____
Address of driver of other vehicle _____33_____
License No. of driver of other vehicle _____34_____
Other driver male or female _____35_____
BUS OPERATOR IDENTIFYING INFORMATION: PASS # _36_ BADGE # _37_ LICENSE NO.-38

21. Which of the following should be entered in Space 4?   21.____
    A. B67   B. 12   C. 7026   D. 10346K

22. Which of the following should be entered in Space 12?   22.____
    A. North   B. South   C. East   D. West

23. Which of the following should be entered in Space 16?   23.____
    A. 10   B. 12   C. 15   D. 67

24. Which of the following should be entered in Space 24?   24.____
    A. 62   B. 67   C. 68   D. 2354

25. Which of the following should be entered in Space 28?   25.____
    A. Red   B. Blue   C. Yellow   D. Green

26. Which of the following should be entered in Space 32?   26.____
    A. Martha Ryan   B. Mary Ryan
    C. George Ryan   D. John Hawkins

27. Which of the following should be entered in Space 37?   27.____
    A. 2354   B. 5712   C. 51VOM-NY D. 5127

28. An angry passenger scolds bus operator George Smith for not stopping at   28.____
    a bus stop. Smith did not hear the passenger signal, but there was a lot of
    traffic noise and he realizes the passenger might have signaled.

Of the following, the BEST action for the bus operator to take is to
- A. keep driving, say nothing, and stop at the next bus stop for which he hears a signal
- B. stop the bus immediately and let the passenger off
- C. tell the passenger in no uncertain terms to signal clearly in the future and, as a lesson to the passenger, skip the next stop as well
- D. explain that he did not hear a signal and let the passenger off at the next stop

29. As a bus approaches a crowded bus stop, an elderly passenger sitting with a cane near the front of the bus rings the bell to get off.
Which of the following is the BEST action for the bus operator to take?
    - A. Stop short of the bus stop, let the elderly passenger out the front door, then pull into the bus stop
    - B. Pull into the bus stop, open the front and rear doors, and tell the elderly passenger to walk to the rear door to get off
    - C. Pull into the bus stop, open the doors, and tell the crowd, *Please let this passenger off*
    - D. Pull into the bus stop, let the crowd on first, then permit the elderly passenger to get out the front door

29.____

30. At an intersection with no traffic control device, which of the following has the right-of-way over the others? A
    - A. pedestrian in the crosswalk
    - B. vehicle making a right turn
    - C. vehicle approaching the intersection
    - D. bus crossing the intersection

30.____

Questions 31-35.

DIRECTIONS: Questions 31 through 35 are to be answered SOLELY on the basis of the Exclusive Lane Rules printed below.

EXCLUSIVE LANE RULES

Bus operators using the exclusive bus and taxi lane westbound to the Howard Tunnel in the eastbound roadway of the Porter Expressway should be guided by the following rules:
1. Headlights must be turned on just before entering the bus lane.
2. Speed must not exceed 35 miles per hour. Police will enforce this limit.
3. At least a 200-foot spacing must be maintained behind the vehicle ahead.
4. If a traffic cone is in the lane, drive over it. Do not attempt to go around it and do not stop your bus.
5. Lane hours are only from 7:00 A.M. to 10:00 A.M. Do not enter at any other time or if the lane is closed.
6. Do not leave the lane at any time, not even to pass a disabled vehicle, except under police direction.
7. Do not open doors or discharge passengers from a disabled bus until police assistance has arrived.

8. Any Transit Authority bus in the exclusive lane able to accommodate discharged passengers from a disabled bus of <u>any</u> company will do so without requiring payment of additional fare.

31. Transit Authority Bus Operator James Hanzelik is operating his bus in the exclusive bus and taxi lane. He is carrying 25 passengers and has room for about 40 more. Hanzelik comes upon an Antelope Bus Company bus which has broken down in front of him in his lane. The Antelope bus has 20 passengers in it. Hanzelik stops his bus. A short time later, a police officer arrives on the scene.
Bus operator Hanzelik should pass the disabled bus under the direction of the police officer after first
    A. taking on the passengers from the disabled bus without charge
    B. taking on the passengers of the disabled bus and charging each of them the difference between the Transit Authority fare and the Antelope Bus Company fare
    C. politely declining to take on the passengers of the disabled bus because it is not a Transit Authority bus
    D. taking on the passengers of the disabled bus and charging each of them the regular Transit Authority fare

31.____

32. You are driving a bus in the exclusive bus and taxi lane. If you observe a traffic cone in the middle of your lane, you should
    A. stop your bus and place the traffic cone where it belongs
    B. go around the traffic cone to avoid destroying it
    C drive over the traffic cone
    D. call for the police to move the traffic cone

32.____

33. Bus Operator Peter Globe is traveling in the exclusive bus and taxi lane when his bus becomes disabled. He stops his bus in the lane and phones for police assistance. While he is waiting for the police to arrive, another bus in the same lane pulls up behind him. The second bus has enough room to accommodate his passengers. After consulting with the other bus operator, he transfers his passengers to the second bus without charging an additional fare.
Bus Operator Globe's action was
    A. *proper*, because the other bus had sufficient room to accommodate his passengers
    B. *improper*, because he transferred the passengers without police assistance
    C. *proper*, because both buses stayed in the exclusive lane
    D. *improper*, because he did not charge his passengers an additional fare

33.____

34. A bus operator driving his bus legally in the exclusive bus and taxi lane should have his headlights on
    A. only when he is passing another vehicle
    B. only when the driver ahead is driving too slowly
    C. if his speed exceeds 35 miles per hour
    D. at all times

34.____

35. Bus Operator Hector Gonzalez is driving his bus in the exclusive bus lane when he has to stop because of a disabled auto blocking his way. The auto had been traveling eastbound in the next lane but got a flat tire and came to a stop in the exclusive lane. Gonzalez waits until the police arrive to guide him around the disabled auto. After the police guide Gonzalez around the disabled auto, they leave. In order to reach the Howard Tunnel before 10:00 A.M., bus operator Gonzalez drives at 40 miles an hour and keeps a distance of 250 feet behind a taxi. He arrives at the Howard Tunnel without incident.
His action was
   A. *proper*, because the lane hours are from 7:00 A.M. to 10:00 A.M.
   B. *improper*, because his speed exceeded 35 miles per hour
   C. *proper*, because he made up for lost time in maintaining his schedule
   D. *improper*, because he should not have waited for the police to guide him

35.____

KEY (CORRECT ANSWERS)

1.	C	11.	C	21.	C	31.	A
2.	B	12.	B	22.	C	32.	C
3.	A	13.	C	23.	C	33.	B
4.	A	14.	C	24.	C	34.	D
5.	C	15.	C	25.	D	35.	B
6.	A	16.	C	26.	A		
7.	C	17.	A	27.	B		
8.	C	18.	B	28.	D		
9.	D	19.	B	29.	C		
10.	D	20.	C	30.	A		

TEST 2

DIRECTIONS: Each question or incomplete statement is followed by several suggested answers or completions. Select the one that BEST answers the question or completes the statement. *PRINT THE LETTER OF THE CORRECT ANSWER IN THE SPACE AT THE RIGHT.*

Questions 1-2.

DIRECTIONS: Questions 1 and 2 are to be answered SOLELY on the basis of the information contained in the following two rules.

1. Bus operators must be relieved only at designated relief points and at the same time specified in schedules, unless otherwise instructed by the proper authority. They must never leave their bus until properly relieved, and must not, under any circumstances, surrender the bus to another employee apparently unfit for duty

2. If a passenger becomes disorderly, annoying, or dangerous, this passenger must be asked to leave the bus at the next designated bus stop.

1. Bus Operator Herbert Bacon is worried about his teenaged daughter who underwent a serious operation. He wants to phone his wife at the hospital to find out how his daughter is feeling. At a designated bus stop, he parks the bus and goes into a tobacco store to use the public telephone.
His action was
   A. *proper*, because he parked in a designated bus stop
   B. *improper*, because he left the bus with no bus operator in charge
   C. *proper*, because the nature of the situation justified the phone call
   D. *improper*, because he could have used a telephone in the street

1.____

2. Bus Operator Wendy Green notices that a passenger who is obviously drunk is annoying the other passengers with his loud and embarrassing remarks. She asks him several times to be quiet, but he continues to bother the passengers. Bus operator Green should stop the bus _____ and ask the drunken passenger to get off.
   A. immediately
   B. at the next dispatcher's station
   C. at the next red light
   D. at the next designated bus stop

2.____

3. Oak Street is one-way northbound and is intersected by Elm Street, which is one-way eastbound.
If there are no traffic control devices at the intersection, and if traffic allows, it should be permissible to make a
   A. right turn from Elm Street into Oak Street
   B. right turn from Oak Street into Elm Street
   C. left turn from Oak Street into Elm Street
   D. four corner U-turn at the intersection

3.____

Questions 4-11.

DIRECTIONS: Questions 4 through 11 are to be answered by consulting the Bus Map on the following page. Notice that the left edge of the map is divided into spaces with letters and the bottom edge of the map is divided into spaces with numbers. The lines for a space with a letter and the lines for a space with a number if extended across the map would meet and form a quadrant (or area). As an example, look at the sketch below which represents part of the map and note that the quadrant formed by an extension of the lines which are boundaries of the F space and of the 2 space meet to form the F2 quadrant. In this quadrant on your map, you can find Lutheran Medical Center. The locations referred to in the questions below can be found within the quadrants shown in parentheses.

4. Which bus route goes from Brooklyn Terminal Market (quadrant F6) to Dyker 4.____
   Beach Park (quadrant H2)?
   A. 78   B. 8   C. 70   D. 7

5. Which route goes from Pratt Institute (quadrant D4) to McCarren Park 5.____
   (quadrant B5)?
   A. 62   B. 38   C. 48   D. 61

6. Which bus should you take to go from Kingsborough Community College 6.____
   (quadrant J5) to Owls Head Park (quadrants F1 and F2)?
   A. 1   B. 4   C. 9   D. 49

7. Which bus route goes from Brooklyn College (quadrant G5) to the intersection 7.____
   of 49th Street and 8th Avenue (quadrant F3)?
   A. 6   B. 11   C. 44   D. 70

8. Which bus route goes from the intersection of 79th Street and Kings Highway 8.____
   (quadrant H3) to Brooklyn College (quadrant G5)?
   A. 6   B. 14   C. 38   D. 52

9. Which bus route goes from the intersection of Flushing Avenue and Nostrand 9.____
   Avenue (quadrant C5) to the intersection of Nostrand Avenue and Quentin
   Road (quadrant H5)?
   A. 100   B. 62   C. 48   D. 44

10. Which bus route goes from the intersection of Empire Blvd. and Rogers Avenue 10.____
    (quadrant E5) to the intersection of Myrtle Avenue and Throop Avenue
    (quadrant C5)?
    A. 44   B. 47   C. 49   D. 54

11. Which bus route goes from the intersection of Ovington Avenue and Fifth 11.____
    Avenue (quadrant G2) to the intersection of 86th Street and Bay Parkway
    (quadrant H3)?
    A. 1   B. 6   C. 5   D. 63

Questions 12-14.

DIRECTIONS: Questions 12 through 14 are to be answered SOLELY on the basis of the following School Bus Bulletin.

SCHOOL BUS BULLETIN

Anywhere in the state, including the city, when the red lights of a school bus flash, you must stop your vehicle before reaching the bus. This is the law, whether you are approaching the bus from the front, or overtaking it from the rear. In fact, you must stop even if the school bus is on the far side of a four-lane divided highway. Children might cross the road after getting off or before getting on the school bus, and they don't always stop to check in both directions before crossing. They depend on you, the motorist, to stop as the law requires. If the red lights of a school bus are flashing, you may pass it only if the school bus clearly signals you to do so, or if you are directed to do so by a police officer.

12. It is evening rush hour during a very hot day. The bus you are operating is 15 minutes behind schedule because of very heavy traffic. The air conditioning system in your bus has broken down, and your passengers are uncomfortable, annoyed, and anxious to get home. You are on a wide, two-way street, and you approach a school bus which is parked with its red lights flashing on the other side of the street. The school bus driver is at the wheel, but you see no children in the bus or anywhere on the street.
    Under the circumstances, you should _____ the school bus.
    A. proceed with caution past
    B. proceed with normal speeding past
    C. stop your bus before reaching
    D. radio for a police officer to direct you past

13. You are a bus operator on a two-lane, one-way main street. You are in the left lane stopped in back of an automobile at a red light. In the lane to your right and in front of you is a school bus which is also waiting for the red light to change. There is no police officer at the corner. When the light changes to green, the car in front of you moves through the intersection, but the school bus stalls and will not start. It does not flash its red lights.
    Under the circumstances, you may
    A. *pass* the school bus because its red lights are not flashing
    B. *not pass* the school bus because there may be children in it
    C. *pass* the school bus only if the school bus driver signals for you to do so
    D. *not pass* the school bus because there is no police officer on the scene

14. You are operating a Transit Authority bus on a one-way street. You approach a school bus from the rear. It is parked at the right curb with its red lights flashing. The school bus is almost filled with children, although a few more are waiting on the sidewalk to get on. After you stop your bus, the school bus driver, who is seated at the wheel of his bus, signals you to pass on the left.
    Under the circumstances, it would be
    A. *proper* for you to pass the school bus because its driver signaled for you to do so
    B. *improper* for you to pass the school bus because children were still boarding
    C. *proper* for you to pass the school bus because most of the children were already inside the bus
    D. *improper* for you to pass the school bus because its red lights were flashing

Questions 15-17.

DIRECTIONS: Questions 15 through 17 are to be answered SOLELY on the basis of the Bulletin shown below.

COLORS OF MONTHLY ELEMENTARY AND REDUCED FARE SCHOOL TICKETS – SUMMER 2021

For the summer of 2021, the colors of the tickets for the School Fare Program for school children will be as follows:

Monthly Elementary School Tickets
Elementary pass FREE – no payment of fare required
July – Blue with Blue Date
August – Rose with Blue Date

High School Eligibility Cards
Students will pay 50 cents going to school in the A.M. and 50 cents on the return trip from school in the P.M. the entire Summer Session.
July – Beige (Green S)
August – Yellow (Green S)

Type #2(r) & #3(c) Rapid Transit Surface Extension
High school students presenting reduced fare passes for all Rapid Transit Surface Extension Routes – B/42, B/54, B/35, BX/55, and Q/49 will be required to pay $1 in the A.M. on the way to school for the entire Summer Session, July 6, 2021 through August 14, 2021.

15. Joe is a second-year high school student attending the Summer Session.
    If he boards a bus on Wednesday, July 23, he
    A. can ride free if he has a valid Blue ticket with Blue Date
    B. must pay 50 cents and show a Beige (Green S) card
    C. must pay 50 cents and show a Blue (Green S) card
    D. must pay 50 cents and show a Yellow (Green S) card

16. Mary is a senior in high school attending the Summer Session.
    When she boards the Surface Extension Route B/54 on her way to taking the train to school, she must show her reduced fare pass and pay
    A. no fare   B. 50¢   C. $1   D. $7.50

17. George, a junior in high school, and his brother, Tyrone, in 5th grade, are both attending the Summer Session.
    If they board a bus on Tuesday, August 4th, the bus operator should look for a _____ ticket and a _____ card.
    A. rose; yellow
    B. blue; beige
    C. blue; blue
    D. rose; beige

18. You are a bus operator driving your bus at normal route speed. Suddenly, a man in a sportscar cuts sharply in front of you and continues to speed away from you.
Which of the following actions would it be BEST for you to take now?
    A. Accelerate to catch up to the sportscar, then cut it off
    B. Get the license number of the sportscar and radio a report to the police
    C. Slow down until the sportscar is at least a quarter mile ahead of you
    D. Continue along your route at normal speed

Questions 19-21.

DIRECTIONS: Questions 19 through 21 are to be answered SOLELY on the basis of the Reverse Bus Movement Procedure shown below.

REVERSE BUS MOVEMENT PROCEDURE

Bus operators may operate a bus in reverse only if they determine that no other turn or movement is possible. When operating in reverse, bus operators must follow all of the following steps in this procedure.

1. The movement in reverse must not be made until the bus operator has walked around to the back of the bus and made a visual inspection of the area behind the bus.
2. The bus operator must be guided by a responsible person, such as a police officer or another bus driver.
3. The person guiding the bus operator must station himself near the left rear of the bus.
4. When the bus operator has determined that it is safe to back up, he will signal by giving three toots of the horn immediately before starting the reverse movement.

19. Bus operator Charles Waters has stopped directly behind a disabled bus and cannot move around the bus without backing up. Waters remains in his seat and asks a police officer to stand at the left rear of the bus to direct him. Waters toots his torn three times and slowly backs up just enough to go around the disabled bus.
Bus operator Waters' actions in backing up the bus were IMPROPER because Waters
    A. was not guided back by a responsible person
    B. should have gotten permission from a supervisor before backing up
    C. tooted his horn just before backing up
    D. did not inspect the area behind the bus before backing up

20. Bus operator Elaine Strollin determines that it is necessary to operate her bus in reverse. She inspects the area to the rear of her bus and determines that it is safe to back up. She toots her horn three times to attract the attention of a police officer to assist her in backing up the bus. The police officer goes to the proper position to direct operator Strollin. With the passengers still in her bus, operator Strollin is directed by the police officer and backs up her bus without incident.

Operator Strollin's actions in backing up the bus were
- A. *proper*, because she had followed the complete procedure for a reverse bus movement
- B. *improper*, because she did not discharge her passengers before backing up
- C. *proper*, because with a police officer present, the complete procedure for a reverse bus movement need not be followed
- D. *improper*, because she did not toot her horn three times just before backing up

21. A bus operator has decided that he must back up his bus. The operator has asked a responsible person to guide his bus back.
Where should he ask that person to stand?
   - A. In front of the bus
   - B. On the right side of the bus near the front door
   - C. At the left rear of the bus
   - D. At the right rear of the bus

21.____

22. A careful driver should allow 20 feet of stopping room for each ten miles an hour of speed. When driving at night, you should be able to stop within the roadway distance illuminated by your headlights.
If your headlights illuminate the roadway approximately 90 feet before you, your speed at night should NOT exceed about _____ miles per hour.
   - A. 25
   - B. 35
   - C. 45
   - D. 55

22.____

Questions 23-24.

DIRECTIONS: Questions 23 and 24 are to be answered on the basis of the following bulletin.

The Culture Bus Loops operate on Saturdays, Sundays, and some holidays. The buses on Culture Bus Loop I (M41) run on the loop through midtown and uptown Manhattan every 30 minutes during the winter and every 20 minutes during the summer, from 10:00 A.M. to 6:00 P.M., and makes 22 stops. You may get off at any one of the stops, take in the sights, and then catch a later bus, or you can simply stay on the bus for the entire loop. Culture Bus Loop II (B88) provides another view of New York City, one that includes midtown and lower Manhattan, and some of Brooklyn as well. The buses on this loop run every 30 minutes, from 9:00 A.M. to 6:00 P.M. Running time is approximately 2 hours and 25 minutes. Tickets for the Culture Buses may be bought only on the buses. Since the driver cannot make change, and since our fare boxes will not accept paper currency, please have your $2.50 fare in any combination of silver or tokens and silver. The Culture Bus Loop I ticket is valid for certain transfer privileges to crosstown buses. By using the crosstown buses, you may tailor your day's itinerary. The Culture Bus Loop I ticket is also valid as an extension to and from the Cloisters on the M4 bus from Stop 10.

23. The Culture Loop II Bus (B88) goes into which borough or boroughs?
   - A. Brooklyn and Manhattan
   - B. Brooklyn and Queens
   - C. Manhattan only
   - D. Manhattan and the Bronx

23.____

8 (#2)

24. The Culture Bus Loop I ticket is also valid on the M4 bus as an extension to and from   24.____
    A. Brooklyn Heights
    B. the Cloisters
    C. Greenwich Village
    D. Staten Island

25. A bus that is traveling at 22 MPH with 30 passengers has a green light as it approaches an intersection. Just as the bus enters the intersection, the light changes from green to yellow.   25.____
    Which of the following is the BEST action for the bus operator to take?
    A. Stop short, back his bus out of the intersection, wait for the light to turn green again, then drive through the intersection
    B. Stop quickly, wait in the intersection for the light to turn green again, then drive through the intersection
    C. Continue through the intersection at 22 MPH
    D. Speed up to get through the intersection before the light turns red

26. You are driving your bus down a one-way street during the rush hour, and you are already 5 minutes behind schedule. You find that you must stop your bus because the street is blocked by a parcel delivery truck which is double-parked, and the driver is not in sight.   26.____
    Which of the following is the FIRST action you should take?
    A. Try to attract the attention of the truck driver by blowing your horn
    B. Back the bus out of the street
    C. Radio the police for a tow truck to come and haul away the parcel delivery truck
    D. Jump out of the bus and knock on the door of the house nearest to the parked truck

27. A bus operator is behind schedule. He has closed his doors and is about to pull out of a bus stop and cross an intersection. The green light is about to change. An elderly man raps on the door of the bus. The operator realizes that if he opens the door for the man to board, he will miss the light and get further behind schedule.   27.____
    Which of the following is the BEST action for the bus operator to take?
    A. Pull away from the bus stop and continue on his route
    B. Go through the intersection before the light changes, then wait for the elderly man to cross the street and board his bus
    C. Open the door and let the man board the bus
    D. Open the door, let the man onto the bus, and tell the man he should have waited for the next bus

Questions 28-29.

DIRECTIONS: Questions 28 and 29 are to be answered SOLELY on the basis of the information contained in the bulletin shown on the following page on Air Pollution.

AIR POLLUTION

No bus operator should permit the gasoline or diesel engine of his bus to discharge air-polluting gases while the bus is stationary at a route terminal. Operators must shut off bus engines, unless otherwise directed, immediately upon completing arrival at the terminal stop. All operators and supervisors should remain constantly alert for any Transit Authority vehicles emitting excessive fumes while in motion. They should report such vehicles immediately on their bus radios to Surface Control by bus number, together with any further available identifying information.

28. Nathan Pearl, a bus operator, is driving his bus along Flatbush Avenue when he black smoke being discharged from the exhaust of a bus coming in the opposite direction.
    Of the following, what should bus operator Pearl do?
    A. Let the bus operator of the other bus take care of it
    B. Tell the other operator about the pollution when he sees him in the garage after they have completed their runs
    C. Call Surface Control to report the bus which is emitting black smoke
    D. Write a report on the bus emitting black smoke when he completes his run, giving the bus number and other identifying information

29. To avoid air pollution, bus operators are ordered to do which of the following?
    A. Drive no more than 12 miles an hour
    B. Shut off the engine at bus stops where a large number of passengers are boarding and alighting
    C. Shut off the engine at terminal stops
    D. Close all windows of the bus so that passengers will not breathe in smoke or fumes being emitted by the bus

30. A bus operator notices a wallet on the floor next to the driver's seat. While waiting at the next red light, he examines the contents of the wallet. It has $30 worth of bills and various cards identifying the owner as Charles Bergen.
    Of the following, it would be MOST appropriate for the bus operator to
    A. hold onto the wallet during the run and return it if a passenger tells him he has lost his wallet and identifies himself as Charles Bergen.
    B. ask passengers if anyone has lost a wallet, and then return the wallet if a person who identifies himself as Charles Bergen claims to have lost the wallet and can identify its contents
    C. pocket the money and inconspicuously place the wallet back on the floor. Anyone careless enough to drop his wallet deserves no sympathy
    D. ask if anyone on the bus has lost a wallet with $30 cash and return it if someone claims to have lost it

31. You are a bus operator. While you are stopped at a red light, a woman onboard your bus, speaking English with a heavy foreign accent, asks you for directions. You do not understand her question.
    Of the following, you should
    A. ask the woman to repeat her question more slowly
    B. ask one of the other passengers to give directions to the woman

C. hand the woman a bus map of the borough you are in
D. give the woman the phone number of the Transit Authority Travel Information Bureau

32. As you are driving your bus, you notice that traffic is close behind you. On a sidewalk about 150 feet ahead of you, some children are playing with a small rubber ball. Suddenly, the ball rolls into the street in the path of your bus. Which of the following actions should you take?
    A. Brake lightly, honk your horn, and be prepared to stop short if a child races after the ball
    B. Honk your horn and stop short in anticipation that one of the children might run after the ball
    C. Honk your horn and continue at normal speed, but be prepared to brake quickly
    D. Honk your horn, then speed up so as to get past the children as quickly as possible

33. Your bus is 15 minutes behind schedule. The bus scheduled to follow your has gotten ahead of you and is in the next bus stop. You wish to pass this bus. As you approach the bus stop, you notice that this bus is starting to pull out.
    You should
    A. honk your horn and pass the bus quickly
    B. pull behind the bus and allow it to continue ahead
    C. pull alongside the bus and tell the driver that you would appreciate it if he did not pass you again
    D. make a turn to a lightly traveled parallel street going in your direction, then drive non-stop for several blocks to both pass the bus in front of you and get back on schedule

34. You are carrying 20 passengers in your bus on a one-way two-lane street. You notice that the car ahead of you is weaving erratically in and out of its lane. Of the following, your MOST appropriate course of action is to
    A. keep a big enough distance between the car and your bus to eliminate any possibility of contact
    B. stay close behind the car and keep honking your horn until the driver of the car either pulls over to a curb or turns down a side street
    C. stay as close behind the car as you can and be prepared to signal the first police officer you see
    D. pass the car and speed away from it

35. Your bus is approaching an intersection with the green light in your favor. From the street on your right, a man on a bicycle is approaching the intersection. The man has sufficient time to stop at the intersection.
    Of the following, the BEST action for you to take is to
    A. exercise your right-of-way and cross the intersection at normal speed
    B. stop and wait until you see what the cyclist does
    C. proceed with caution, ready to apply brakes if necessary
    D. accelerate through the light before the cyclist reaches the intersection

KEY (CORRECT ANSWERS)

1.	B	11.	A	21.	C	31.	A
2.	D	12.	C	22.	C	32.	A
3.	B	13.	A	23.	A	33.	B
4.	B	14.	A	24.	B	34.	A
5.	C	15.	B	25.	C	35.	C
6.	A	16.	C	26.	A/C		
7.	B	17.	A	27.	C		
8.	A	18.	D	28.	C		
9.	D	19.	D	29.	C		
10.	B	20.	D	30.	B		

EXAMINATION SECTION
TEST 1

DIRECTIONS: Each question or incomplete statement is followed by several suggested answers or completions. Select the one that BEST answers the question or completes the statement. *PRINT THE LETTER OF THE CORRECT ANSWER IN THE SPACE AT THE RIGHT.*

Questions 1-5.

DIRECTIONS: Questions 1 through 5 are to be answered on the basis of the Bus Radio Transmission Code shown below.

BUS RADIO TRANSMISSION CODE

Buses are equipped with a two-way radio system to aid the Bus Operator in the performance of his job. It is used primarily to transmit information to the Radio Dispatcher located in the Central Radio Operations Center. To assist the Bus Operator in the transmission of information without loss of time or possible confusion, the following Code is used:

Code Red Tag: To be used only in extreme emergency such as police assistance in the event of a hold-up, assault, serious vandalism, etc. The Bus Operator transmitting a Red Tag alert shall have priority over all other incoming calls. All other Bus Operators shall stand by until Dispatcher gives order to resume normal operations.
Code 1: Collision involving a bus.
Code 2: Passenger injured on board a bus
Code 3: Disabled bus
Code 4: Bus blocked by fire apparatus, other vehicle, parade, etc.

1. If a bus operator observes a mugging take place on his bus, he should radio a Code
   A. 1   B. 2   C. 4   D. Red Tag   1._____

2. If a passenger trips and hurts himself on a bus, the bus operator should radio a Code
   A. 1   B. 2   C. 3   D. Red Tag   2._____

3. If a bus is blocked by a street demonstration of marching adults, the bus operator should radio a Code
   A. 1   B. 2   C. 4   D. Red Tag   3._____

4. While a bus operator is reporting an injury to a passenger who fell and hurt his leg on the bus, a second bus operator interrupts this radio conversation with a Code Red Tag.
   The FIRST bus operator should
   A. continue with his message so that the passenger may be aided quickly
   B. repeat his message since the interruption may have scrambled his voice   4._____

C. immediately stop talking
D. ask the second bus operator to wait until he has completed his message

5. If a bus engine stalls and cannot be restarted, the bus operator should radio a Code
   A. 1 B. 2 C. 3 D. Red Tag

6. When a passenger deposits his fare into the fare box, the coins drop onto a tray. When this tray is tilted by the bus operator, it causes coins to drop into a cash box located beneath the tray. Bus operators are required to tilt the tray after each fare is deposited so that the tray will be empty when the next passenger deposits his fare.
   The MOST logical reason for tilting the tray after each fare is to
   A. show the passengers that the money they deposit is being collected
   B. enable bus operators to see that each passenger deposits the correct fare
   C. prevent passengers from seeing how much money is in the fare box
   D. keep the tilt tray moving all the time so that it doesn't stick

7. An angry passenger getting off a bus at the front door loudly scolds the bus operator for not stopping at the preceding bus stop.
   If the operator knows that the stop signal was not given until the bus was actually passing the preceding bus stop, the BEST action for him to take is to
   A. tell the passenger to wake up and give the stop signal in time
   B. tell the passenger to be quiet and not make a nuisance of himself
   C. call on the rest of the passengers to verify that the complaining passenger did not ring the stop signal in time
   D. avoid getting into an argument with this passenger

8. A bus operator who is waiting on a two-way street to make a left-hand turn onto another street should
   A. turn his front wheels about 45 and keep his foot on the gas pedal
   B. turn his front wheels about 45 and keep his foot on the brake
   C. leave his front wheels facing straight ahead and keep his foot on the gas pedal
   D. leave his front wheels facing straight head and keep his foot on the brake

9. A bus operator notices that a child who is with her mother is playing with the exit signal bell cord.
   In this case, it would be BEST for the bus operator to
   A. ask the mother to stop her child from playing with the bell cord
   B. disconnect the bell cord until the mother and child get off the bus
   C. stop only at those bus stops where people are waiting or when he sees seated passengers on his bus stand up
   D. continue to stop at all bus stops in case someone actually wants to get off the bus

10. A passenger boards a bus and asks a seated passenger to remove his package from a seat so that he may sit down because there are no other empty seats. The seated passenger refuses his request and both passengers start arguing, which creates such a disturbance that the other passengers start complaining. In this situation, the bus operator should
    A. stop the bus until the problem is settled
    B. tell the seated passenger to remove his package
    C. order the seated passenger to pay another fare for the second seat
    D. tell the standing passenger to wait until another seat is available

10.____

11. A woman passenger is not paying attention and suddenly realizes that she has passed her stop. She asks the bus operator to let her off immediately. The bus operator would be using good judgement if he
    A. immediately stops the bus to let the woman off and makes no comment
    B. immediately stops the bus to let the woman off and warns her to be careful
    C. keeps driving and tells her he is only allowed to let her off at the next scheduled stop
    D. keeps driving and says nothing to her

11.____

12. While looking into the rear view mirror, a bus operator sees a man entering the bus from the rear door in order to avoid paying the required bus fare. The bus operator tells the man that he must pay the required fare or get off the bus. If the man agrees to pay the fare, it would be BEST for the operator to
    A. order the man to get off the bus as a penalty for being dishonest
    B. insist that the man pay a double fare for causing a delay
    C. allow the man to ride free but warn him not to try to sneak on again
    D. collect the fare and continue along the bus route as scheduled

12.____

13. During rush hours, a bus operator is proceeding along his bus route with a full bus load of seated and standing passengers when someone rings the bell to get off. As he approaches the next bus stop, he sees a crowd of people waiting to get on the bus.
    In this situation, it would be BEST for the operator to
    A. skip the stop and go directly to the next stop since there is no room for anyone else to enter the bus
    B. pull into the stop so that anyone wishing to get off the bus may do so
    C. go past the bus stop but stop the bus in the middle of the block so that passengers can get off the bus but no one else can get on
    D. pull into the stop and order the people closest to the door to take a transfer ticket and get off the bus to make more standing room

13.____

14. While driving on his route through a narrow street, a bus operator is forced to stop his bus because a large moving van is blocking the way. The driver of the van is jockeying the van back and forth in order to back it into a street-level loading platform. The stopping of the bus has caused cars to accumulate behind it, and the drivers of these cars start to blow their horns.

14.____

In this case, the bus operator should
- A. signal the cars behind to back out of the street
- B. blow his horn also to hurry the van driver
- C. try to find a policeman so he can clear the street
- D. wait until there is sufficient clearance to drive past the van

15. On legal holidays when all public schools, banks, many private businesses, and federal, state, and city offices are closed, the Authority operates a reduced schedule. This mean that buses arrive at bus stops less often because there are fewer buses running.
Of the following, the MOST logical reason for having fewer buses running on legal holidays is that
- A. buses will not be in the way if there are parades on major streets
- B. there are usually fewer passengers riding the buses on legal holidays
- C. more Authority employees will have the day off on legal holidays
- D. the public will show respect for the legal holiday being observed

15.____

Questions 16-18.

DIRECTIONS: Questions 16 through 18 are to be answered on the basis of the explanation on How to Find the Street Nearest a House Number on Any Avenue given below.

HOW TO FIND THE STREET NEAREST A HOUSE NUMBER ON ANY AVENUE

Take the house number, drop the last figure, divide by 2, and add or subtract the key number given in the chart below.

For example: Near what cross street is 500 Fifth Avenue? Drop the last 0, divide the 50 by 2, and you get 25. Add the key number 18, and the result is 43. Therefore, Number 500 Fifth Avenue is nearest to 43rd Street.

Avenue	Key Number
First Ave.	Add 3
Fifth Ave.	Add 18
Sixth Ave.	Subtract 12

Avenue	Key Number
Amsterdam Ave.	Add 600
Lenox Ave.	Add 110
Madison Ave.	Add 26

16. Number 80 Amsterdam Ave. is NEAREST to _____ St.
   A. 20th B. 56th C. 64th D. 100th

16.____

17. Number 260 Sixth Ave. is NEAREST to _____ St.
   A 1st B. 13th C. 16th D. 25th

17.____

18. Number 1064 Madison Ave. is NEAREST to _____ St.
   A. 41st B. 56th C. 63rd D. 79th

18.____

19. Bus operators are not required to wear the official cap during the summer. The badge which is ordinarily worn on the cap, must then be displayed on the right shoulder.

19.____

The MOST likely reason for requiring the wearing of the badge on the right shoulder is that this location
   A. interferes least with the operation of the bus
   B. prevents the badge from being stolen
   C. reassures the passengers that the operator is a good driver
   D. permits easy identification of the operator

20. During snowstorms, bus operators are required to request passengers leaving the bus to *Please Be Careful and Watch Your Step*.
    The MOST likely reason for making this request is to
    A. avoid lawsuits in case of an accident
    B. alert passengers to the danger of slipping
    C. warn the passengers that the rear door is for exit
    D. improve relations with the public

21. Just after the bus operator of a Number 10 bus closes his doors at a bus stop, a man hammers with his fist on the front door demanding to get on the bus. After the bus operator opens the door, the man gets on and asks if the bus is a Number 15.
    The bus operator would be practicing good public relations if he told the man
    A. to get off and check the number on the front of the bus
    B. that it is not a Number 15 and let the man off the bus
    C. that he cannot answer questions while the bus is in motion
    D. that he cannot answer now since the bus is behind schedule

22. A drunk boards a bus and refuses to pay his fare. While the bus operator is attempting to get the drunk to pay his fare, another passenger deposits the fare for the drunk saying that he is in a hurry.
    The bus operator should
    A. refuse the fare since it was not paid by the proper person
    B. proceed on the way in a normal manner
    C. proceed until he comes upon a policeman and have him arrest the drunk
    D. put the drunk off the bus since he was causing a disturbance

23. A bus operator has requested the passengers to *Move to the Rear, please*, but the passengers continue to obstruct the entrance door even though there is considerable room in the rear of the bus.
    The BEST course of action for the bus operator would be to
    A. stop the bus and tell all passengers to get off the bus
    B. alternately brae and accelerate the bus to shake the passengers to the rear
    C. skip all stops until the passengers move
    D. continue to request that the passengers move to the rear so that others can get on

24. One of the Authority rules regarding lost property is that certain types of property 24.____
should be held for not more than 8 hours and then must be sold or destroyed.
Of the following, the lost property that should come under this rule is a
   A. package of fresh fish	B. bottle of whiskey
   C. suit of clothes	D. a can of peaches

Questions 25-30.

DIRECTIONS: Questions 25 through 30 are to be answered on the basis of the following schedules for Running Time and Headway. Running time is the scheduled time for a bus to travel from one stop to the next. For example, the running time between Twelfth Ave. and Fifteenth Ave. is 7 minutes when traveling Northbound and 8 minutes when traveling Southbound during the hours from 11:00 P.M. to 6:00 A.M.

Headway is the scheduled time between one bus and the next bus, which varies according to the time of day. For example, at Midnight the time between buses is 18 minutes. In answering these questions, refer to these schedules and assume that each bus proceeds on schedule.

Bus Stop	RUNNING TIME			
	11:00 P.M. to 6:00 A.M.		6:00 A.M. to 11:00 P.M.	
	Northbound (going)	Southbound (returning)	Northbound (going)	Southbound (returning)
First Ave.	8	9	12	14
Fourth Ave.	5	6	9	10
Seventh Ave.	9	9	13	13
Ninth Ave.	5	6	9	10
Twelfth Ave.	7	8	11	12
Fifteenth Ave.				

HEADWAY		
From	To	Minutes
6:00 A.M.	9:30 A.M.	5
9:30 A.M.	4:30 P.M.	12
4:30 P.M.	6:00 P.M.	4
6:00 P.M.	11:00 P.M.	15
11:00 P.M.	6:00 P.M.	18

25. The bus leaving Fourth Ave., Northbound, at 11:30 A.M. is scheduled to arrive 25.____
at Ninth Ave. at _____ A.M.
   A. 11:44	B. 11:45	C. 11:51	D. 1:52

26. The bus leaving Fifteenth Ave., Southbound, at 4:28 A.M. is scheduled to 26.____
arrive at First Ave. at _____ A.M.
   A. 5:02	B. 5:06	C. 5:22	D. 5:27

27. If a passenger starting at First Ave. wanted to be at Twelfth Ave. by 12 Noon, he should board a bus that leaves no later than _____ A.M.
    A. 11:17   B. 11:19   C. 11:22   D. 11:23

28. At 10:0 P.M., a man who wants to board a bus at the corner of Fourth Ave. sees the bus pull away from the curb.
    For the NEXT bus, he should have a wait of _____ minutes.
    A. 5   B. 12   C. 15   D. 18

29. A bus which is on schedule becomes disabled at the Seventh Ave. bus stop at 11:45 A.M.
    The NEXT scheduled bus should arrive at this stop at
    A. 11:49 A.M.   B. 11:50 A.M.   C. 11:57 A.M.   D. 12 Noon

30. A passenger who takes a bus at 8:30 A.M. usually arrives at work six or seven minutes late. He is supposed to be at work at 9:00 A.M.
    In order NOT to be late, he should take a bus which leaves his stop _____ minutes earlier.
    A. 5   B. 7   C. 10   D. 12

KEY (CORRECT ANSWERS)

1. D	11. C	21. B
2. B	12. D	22. B
3. C	13. B	23. D
4. C	14. D	24. A
5. C	15. B	25. D
6. B	16. C	26. B
7. D	17. A	27. A
8. D	18. D	28. C
9. A	19. D	29. C
10. B	20. B	30. C

TEST 2

DIRECTIONS: Each question or incomplete statement is followed by several suggested answers or completions. Select the one that BEST answers the question or completes the statement. *PRINT THE LETTER OF THE CORRECT ANSWER IN THE SPACE AT THE RIGHT.*

Questions 1-5.

DIRECTIONS: Questions 1 through 5 are to be answered on the basis of the following bulletin on School Eligibility Cards. In answering these questions, refer to this bulletin.

SCHOOL ELIGIBILITY CARDS

All bus operators are responsible for the proper use of School Eligibility Cards for reduced fares on their buses. These cards are issued to elementary and high school students. Such cards are good for the entire year from September 13 to June 28 next and are issued subject to the following conditions:

1. The card is to be used by the student whose name appears on the face of the card, and only on days when school is in session. If offered by any other person, it will be taken away by the bus operator and full fare will be collected from the person presenting the card.
2. The card will allow the student to ride on the particular bus indicated on the face of the card for a fare of fifty cents between 6 A.M. and 7 P.M. The fare of fifty cents must be deposited in the fare box by the student after the card is shown to the bus operator.
3. The student, after paying the fifty-cent fare, is entitled to the same transfer privileges as other passengers.
4. The card will be taken away if altered or misused, and the student will not be given a new card for a period of five school months.
5. The card is not good unless all entries on the card are made by the teacher and the card is signed by the teacher.

1. If a sudent's School Eligibility Card is taken away by a bus operator because of misuse, the student will
   A. never be issued a new card because of this misuse
   B. not be issued a new card until he pays for the old one
   C. be eligible for a new card after five school months
   D. be eligible for a new card if he gets a note from his teacher

1.____

2. A bus operator should take away a School Eligibility Card if it is presented
   A. at 9 A.M. before school opens   B. at 3 P.M. after school opens
   C. by a college student   D. more than twice a day

2.____

3. A bus operator should permit a student to ride at reduced fare if he presents his School Eligibility Card at
   A. 8:00 A.M. on Sunday   B. 8:00 A.M. on Monday
   C. 8:00 P.M. on Saturday   D. 8:00 P.M. on Wednesday

3.____

4. If a student presents a School Eligibility Card, pays a fifty-cent fare, and asks   4.____
   for a transfer, the bus operator should
   A. tell the student that during school hours he may not get a transfer
   B. tell him to use his School Eligibility Card instead
   C. give him a transfer if other passengers can get them free
   D. tell him he must pay the full $1.00 fare to get one

5. According to the above bulletin, School Eligibility Cards are NOT good on   5.____
   A. September 15   B. October 26
   C. February 23 next   D. June 30 next

Questions 6-15.

DIRECTIONS: Questions 6 through 15 are to be answered on the basis of the Bus Operator's Daily Trip Sheet shown below, which was turned in by a bus operator after the completion of his trip. At the control points shown, the bus operator made entries on this Trip Sheet after taking readings of the cash counter and the token counter, which are part of his fare box. These counters show the number of tokens collected and the total value of the coins placed in the fare box. Between the control points, the bus operator also noted the number of transfers he had collected and the number of children using students' bus passes since the last control point. Assume that all passengers were picked up at bus stops between control points and that students using bus passes were not required to pay an additional fare. Assume a fare of $1.00 and no charge for transfers.

BUS OPERATOR'S DAILY TRIP SHEET							
Control Point	Leaves At	Counter Readings				Transfers Collected	Students' Bus Passes
		Cash	Difference	Tokens	Difference		
Filmore Ave.	10:08 AM	0	$9.00	0	2	1	0
Flatlands Ave.	10:23 AM	$9.00	$24.00	2	3	4	2
Kings Highway	10:59 AM	$33.00	$17.00	5	5	0	5
Glenwood Road	11:39 AM	$50.00	$12.00	10	0	2	1
Foster Ave.	12:19 PM	$62.00	$19.00	10	4	3	4
Church Ave.	12:55 PM	$91.00	$14.00	14	1	1	2
Linden Blvd.	1:10 PM	$95.00		15			

6. The scheduled travel time between leaving Filmore Ave. and leaving Flatlands   6.____
   Ave. is _____ minutes.
   A. 10   B. 15   C. 36   D. 40

7. The scheduled travel time between leaving Foster Ave. and leaving Linden   7.____
   Blvd. is _____ minutes.
   A. 36   B. 41   C. 46   D. 51

8. The amount of cash collected between Filmore Ave. and Linden Blvd. was
   A. $14.00   B. $81.00   C. $95.00   D. $110.00

9. The total number of passengers carried between Filmore Ave. and Flatlands Ave. was
   A. 9   B. 10   C. 11   D. 12

10. The total number of tokens collected between Filmore Ave. and Church Ave. was
    A. 2   B. 5   C. 10   D. 14

11. The total number of persons paying a cash fare between Church Ave. and Linden Blvd. was
    A. 14   B. 15   C. 30   D. 95

12. The total number of school children who rode the bus by presenting a students' bus pass between Flatlands Ave. to Linden Blvd. was
    A. 12   B. 13   C. 14   D. 15

13. The total number of passengers carried on the trip from Filmore Ave. to Linden Blvd. was
    A. 76   B. 85   C. 105   D. 135

14. The GREATEST number of passenger paying a cash fare boarded the bus between
    A. Flatlands Ave. and Kings Highway
    B. Kings Highway and Glenwood Road
    C. Glenwood Road and Foster Ave.
    D. Foster Ave. and Church Ave.

15. The GREATEST number of persons got on the bus by use of transfers and students' bus passes and not by payment of a cash fare or tokens between
    A. Kings Highway and Glenwood Road
    B. Glenwood Road and Foster Ave.
    C. Foster Ave. and Church Ave.
    D. Church Ave. and Linden Blvd.

16. After a bus operator opens the doors at a bus stop, the first person on line stands in the doorway and asks for directions. After he receives the directions, the man asks for further details, and the people on the line start to complain about the delay.
    Of the following, it would be BEST for the bus operator to
    A. ask the people in the line to be quiet so that the man can be heard
    B. tell the man to wait for the next bus which will not be as crowded
    C. refuse to give him the information until he pays his fare
    D. give the man the details he requests

17. The rules of the Authority allow bus operators to wear glasses with tinted lenses except before sun-up and after sun-down.
The MOST likely reason for not allowing bus operators to wear tinted glasses before sun-up is that
   A. the bus operator may temporarily be blinded when the sun is coming up
   B. the use of tinted glasses at this time is poor public relations
   C. tinted lenses restrict the bus operator's vision at that time
   D. the passengers may think the bus operator has bad vision

17.____

18. While a bus is stopped for a traffic light at a busy intersection which is not a bus stop, a passenger pulls the cord several times and demands to be let off so he can catch a connecting bus that is passing by.
The BEST course of action for the bus operator would be to
   A. open the door and let the passenger out
   B. signal the connecting bus to wait for the passenger
   C. ignore the passenger
   D. tell the passenger that bus operators are allowed to open the doors only at bus stops

18.____

19. Bus operators are forbidden to operate a bus while their right hand rests on the fare box.
The MOST likely reason for this rule is that resting a hand on the fare box
   A. is unsafe since both hands should be on the steering wheel
   B. prevents the deposit of fares in the fare box
   C. disturbs the passengers since the operator appears too relaxed
   D. may interfere with the forward view of the passengers

19.____

20. A rule of the Authority forbids bus operators from accepting fares by hand and requires that the operator tell the passengers to put their fares in the fare box.
The MOST likely reason for this rule is to
   A. guarantee that all passengers deposit the correct fare
   B. reduce the chances of the fare being dropped onto the floor
   C. make sure that all fares are registered by the fare box
   D. prevent physical contact between the bus operator and the passengers

20.____

21. Passengers are allowed to play radios on Authority buses if the playing of the radio does not disturb other passengers.
If a young man is playing a radio very loudly and getting into arguments with other passengers who are complaining about the noise, the bus operator would be using good judgment if he
   A. tells the young man to turn the radio off completely and that he will be thrown off the bus if he turns it on again
   B. takes the radio away from the young man and tells him he can pick it up at the Authority headquarters
   C. tells the young man to lower the volume of the radio
   D. asks the passengers what radio station they would like to listen to and tells the young man to tune the radio to that station

21.____

22. A passenger boarding a bus has one foot on the bus and one foot still on the sidewalk. He is causing a delay of the bus while he is talking to someone who is not getting on the bus. This has been going on for some time, and the other passengers start complaining about the delay.
Of the following, it would be BEST for the bus operator to
    A. take his foot off the brake pedal and gently ease the bus forward, thereby informing the boarding passenger that he is causing a delay
    B. ignore the passengers who are complaining and allow the boarding passenger to finish his conversation
    C. close the doors halfway and then reopen them in order to force the boarding passenger to either get on or off the bus
    D. tell the boarding passenger that he should step aside and wait for the next bus if he wants to continue his conversation

23. A rule of the Authority states that: *A bus operator shall study maps and literature concerning the area along his bus route and the streets and points of interest nearby.*
Of the following, the BEST reason for this rule is that the bus operator will
    A. be better able to drive his bus in the area
    B. become more interested in his work
    C. be better able to give correct information to passengers asking questions
    D. know how to re-route his bus in case of a tie-up on his regular route

24. Bus operators must carefully inspect their buses before driving them out of the garage. All safety features, including the brakes, must be checked to see that they are in good working order.
The MOST important reason for this regulation is to
    A. provide for the safety of passengers
    B. protect the Authority from paying damages in accident cases
    C. improve the driving abilities of bus operators
    D. give the bus repairman work to do

25. Occasional unpleasant incidents with passengers who are insulting may be annoying to the bus operator.
Keeping this in mind, a newly-appointed bus operator should
    A. be suspicious of all passengers
    B. not be friendly with passengers at any time
    C. discourage passengers from asking questions by giving nasty replies
    D. try to remember the considerate passengers instead of the few inconsiderate ones

KEY (CORRECT ANSWERS)

1. C
2. C
3. B
4. C
5. D

6. B
7. D
8. C
9. D
10. D

11. A
12. C
13. D
14. A
15. C

16. D
17. C
18. D
19. A
20. C

21. C
22. D
23. C
24. A
25. D

EXAMINATION SECTION
TEST 1

DIRECTIONS: Each question or incomplete statement is followed by several suggested answers or completions. Select the one that BEST answers the question or completes the statement. *PRINT THE LETTER OF THE CORRECT ANSWER IN THE SPACE AT THE RIGHT.*

1. Present traffic procedure is to have one lane on man wide one-way streets marked out in yellow paint.
   This line is to be
   A. used by regular vehicles when a siren is heard
   B. cleared for vehicles about to make a left turn
   C. used exclusively by emergency vehicles
   D. cleared for emergency vehicles when a siren to heard

   1.____

2. It is CORRECT to say that a(the)
   A. vehicle may be legally parked 15 feet from a fire hydrant
   B. legal speed limit in the city is 45 miles per hour
   C. distance required to stop at 10 m.p.h. is just half that required at 20 m.p.h.
   D. flashing yellow light means stop and then go

   2.____

3. To stop a motor vehicle on an icy street with the LEAST chance of skidding, the operator should
   A. apply the brakes normally
   B. step on the accelerator lightly after releasing it
   C. make a number of light foot-brake applications
   D. apply the hand brake only

   3.____

4. Transit employees are urged to be courteous to passengers MAINLY to
   A. assure safety   B. maintain bus schedules
   C. win prizes   D. maintain good public relations

   4.____

5. Improper use of the horn of a motor vehicle is not permitted.
   It would be clearly IMPROPER for a bus operator to sound
   A. several short blasts to warn pedestrian stragglers in front of his bus at an intersection
   B. several short blasts to warn a motorist about to pull away from the curb in front of a moving bus
   C. three short blasts as a warning before he backs up
   D. two short blasts as he is passing another bus going in the opposite direction

   5.____

6. A recognized principle in good urban transportation is that the interval between buses at any particular time of day should be uniform.
   The MOST likely consequence of an unusually long time gap between buses resulting from traffic conditions is

   6.____

A. heavy riding on some buses
B. confusion of passengers
C. crossing accidents
D. loss of regular patronage

7. It is an indication of a safe driver if the operator
   A. *seldom* yields the right-of-way
   B. *seldom* runs ahead of schedule
   C. *frequently* yields the right-of-way
   D. *frequently* runs behind schedule

8. A person who has been a rider on buses can reason that the failure which would LEAST likely be the cause for a bus being taken out of service is a _____ door stuck _____.
   A. rear; closed
   B. front; closed
   C. rear; open
   D. front; open

Questions 9-18.

DIRECTIONS: Questions 9 through 18 are to be answered on the basis of the following description of an incident. Read the description carefully before answering these questions.

DESCRIPTION OF INCIDENT

On Tuesday, October 8, at about 4:00 P.M., Bus Operator Sam Bell, Badge No. 3871, whose accident record was perfect, was operating his half-filled bus, No. 4392Y northbound and on schedule along Dean Street. At this time, a male passenger who was apparently intoxicated started to yell and to use loud and profane language. The bus driver told this passenger to be quiet or to get off the bus. The passenger said that he would not be quiet but indicated that he wanted to get off the bus by moving toward the front door exit. When he reached the front of the bus, which at the time was in motion, the intoxicated passenger slapped the bus operator on the back and pulled the steering wheel sharply. This action caused the bus to sideswipe a passenger automobile coming from the opposite direction before the operator could stop the bus. The sideswiped car was a red 2004 Pontiac 2-door convertible, License 6416-KN, driven by Albert Holt. The bus driver kept the doors of his bus closed and blew the horn vigorously. The horn blowing was quickly answered as Sergeant Henry Burns, Badge No. 1208, and Patrolman Joe Cross, Badge No. 24643, happened to be following a few cars behind the bus in police car No. 736. The intoxicated passenger, who gave his name as John Doe, was placed under arrest, and Patrolman Cross took the names of witnesses while Sergeant Burns recorded the necessary vehicular information. Investigation showed that no one was injured in the accident and that the entire damage to the automobile was having its side slightly pushed in.

9. From the information given, it can be reasoned that
   A. it was just beginning to rain
   B. Dean Street is a two-way street
   C. there were mostly women shoppers on the bus
   D. most seats in the bus were filled

3 (#1)

10. The name of the policeman who was riding in the police car with the sergeant was
    A. Cross   B. Bell   C. Holt   D. Burns

11. From the description, it is evident that the passenger automobile was traveling
    A. north   B. south   C. east   D. west

12. It is logical to conclude that the passenger automobile was damaged on its
    A. front end   B. rear end   C. right side   D. left side

13. A fact concerning the intoxicated passenger that is clearly stated in the above description is that he
    A. was intoxicated when he got on the bus
    B. hit a fellow passenger
    C. pulled the steering wheel sharply
    D. was not arrested

14. The bus operator called the attention of the police by
    A. sideswiping an oncoming car
    B. yelling and using profane language
    C. blowing his horn vigorously
    D. stopping a police car coming from the opposite direction

15. A reasonable conclusion that can be drawn from the above description is that
    A. the name John Doe was fictitious
    B. the sideswiped automobile was from out of town
    C. some of the passengers on the bus were injured
    D. the bus operator tried to put the intoxicated passenger off the bus

16. The number of the police car involved in the incident was
    A. 4392Y   B. 6416-KN   C. 1208   D. 736

17. From the facts stated, it is obvious that the bus operator was
    A. behind schedule
    B. driving too close to the center of the street
    C. discourteous to the intoxicated passenger
    D. a good driver

18. It is clearly stated that the
    A. sideswiped automobile was a blue sedan
    B. bus driver kept the bus doors closed until the police came
    C. incident happened on a Thursday
    D. police sergeant took down the names of witnesses

19. At terminals in residential areas where a bus remains for more than 3 minutes, operators are required to turn off their engines.
    The LEAST important reason for stopping the engines is to
    A. reduce noise   B. conserve fuel
    C. reduce air pollution   D. minimize engine wear

20. Statistics show that automobile accidents occur MOST frequently 20.____
    A. in the morning rush hours   B. around noon
    C. soon after sunset   D. near midnight

21. A bus operator is liable under the law to receive a traffic ticket for 21.____
    A. double standing when a bus stop is occupied by a car
    B. not taking on all people waiting at a stop
    C. passing a preceding bus on a grade
    D. discharging a passenger at other than a bus stop

22. A bus operator approaching a green light sees a pedestrian crossing his path 22.____
    against the light.
    If the pedestrian is two or three bus lengths away, the operator
    A. is required to make a complete stop
    B. should swing his bus closer to the curb
    C. is required to report the pedestrian to the nearest police officer
    D. should reduce his speed and blow his horn

23. The power to revoke a license to drive a motor vehicle is in the hands of the 23.____
    A. Police Commissioner   B. Traffic Commissioner
    C. Commissioner of Motor Vehicles D. Mayor

24. When passing a playground, park or other area where children are playing or 24.____
    walking,
    A. stop and then proceed with caution
    B. slow down and proceed with caution
    C. blow horn and make sure they see you
    D. blow horn, stop, and then proceed with caution

Questions 25-34.

DIRECTIONS: Questions 25 through 34 are to be answered on the basis of the following sketch showing the routes of the Grand Avenue (solid line) and the Elm St. (dotted line) buses. Refer to this sketch when answering these questions.

5 (#1)

25. A bus on Alp St. going to the Cort St. terminal is moving 25.____
    A. north   B. east   C. south   D. west

26. If the distance around a terminal loop is one-half mile, the total distance that 26.____
    a bus must travel in one roundtrip between the Dey Ave. and Roe St. terminals,
    including both terminal loops is NEAREST to _____ miles.
    A. 26.1   B. 26.7   C. 27.2   D. 28.4

27. One street used by buses operating in both directions is 27.____
    A. Taft Avenue   B. Roe Street   C. Cort Street   D. Nash Avenue

28. The bus route distance between the Elm St. and Cort St. terminals is _____ 28.____
    miles.
    A. 8.6   B. 9.2   C. 9.7   D. 18.9

29. A passenger must transfer if he is going from Dey Ave. terminal to 29.____
    A. Taft Ave.   B. Elm St.   C. Cort St.   D. Park Ave.

30. Buses are NOT required to make even one left turn at the terminal at 30.____
    A. Cort St.   B. Dey Ave.   C. Elm St.   D. Roe St.

31. After discharging all passengers at the Dey Ave. terminal before going around 31.____
    the loop, the number of left turns a bus must make to reach Elm St. is
    A. 1   B. 2   C. 3   D. 4

32. From the Cort St. terminal to Elm St., a bus travels a TOTAL distance of _____ 32.____
    miles.
    A. 5.7   B. 6.0   C. 6.3   D. 7.2

33. If the common rule for estimating distance of 20 blocks to the mile is adhered 33.____
    to, then the number of blocks a bus travels on Grand Ave. is
    A. 56   B. 80   C. 110   D. 136

34. If the timetable calls for a bus to cover the distance along Dey Ave. from the 34.____
    terminal to Kip St. in 12 minutes, the average speed of the bus on this stretch
    must be _____ miles.
    A. 1.1   B. 6.5   C. 10   D. 15.5

35. In the Civilian Defense air raid warning system, a three-minute warbling sound 35.____
    of the sirens is the _____ signal.
    A. alert   B. test   C. all clear   D. take cover

36. If a person should ask you, while on duty in your bus, for directions on how to 36.____
    reach a particular location to which you do not know the answer, your BEST
    course of action is to
    A. tell the person you do not know
    B. give the person the best directions you can think of

C. tell the person to buy a directory
D. explain to the person that the rules prohibit talking to an operator while he is on duty

37. The rules of the Transit Authority state that employees should not make any statements concerning transit accidents except too proper officials of the Transit Authority upon inquiry.
The PROBABLE reason for this rule is to
A. conceal facts that may be damaging
B. avoid conflicting testimony
C. prevent lawsuits
D. prevent unofficial statements from being accepted as official

37.____

38. As a potential bus operator, you should know that when you are about to back a bus, it is NEVER necessary for you to
A. check that there is sufficient room behind the bus
B. signal your intention
C. turn on back-up lights
D. check the brake air pressure

38.____

39. A flashing red traffic signal indicates that a driver
A. must stop and wait until the light stops flashing
B. must stop and then proceed when the way is clear
C. may make a right turn without stopping
D. must yield the right-of-way but does not have to stop

39.____

40. Operators should be instructed that collision accidents at street intersections protected by traffic lights can USUALLY be avoided if they will remember that
A. traffic lights are often out of order
B. a car coming from the right has the right-of-way
C. they can depend on the other drive obeying the lights
D. there is no substitute for an alert driver

40.____

Questions 41-50.

DIRECTIONS: Questions 41 through 50 are to be answered on the basis of the portion of a bus timetable shown below. Refer to this timetable in answering these questions.

TIMETABLE – LAKESIDE LINE – WEEKDAYS

	SOUTHBOUND				NORTHBOUND			
Bus No.	Mack St. Lv.	High St Lv.	Ace St. Lv.	Burr St. Arr.	Burr St. Lv.	Ace St. Lv.	High St. Lv.	Mark St. Arr.
10	6:06	6:14	6:32	6:46	6:55	7:09	7:27	7:35
11	6:21	6:29	6:47	7:01	7:10	7:24	7:42	7:50
12	6:36	6:44	7:02	7:16	7:25	7:39	7:57	6:05
13	6:51	6:59	7:17	7:31	7:40	7:54	8:12	8:20
14	7:03	7:11	7:29	7:43	7:55	8:09	8:27	8:35
15	7:15	7:23	7:41	7:55	8:10	8:24	8:42	8:50
16	7:28	7:36	7:54	8:08	8:25	8:39	8:57	9:05
17	7:41	7:49	8:07	8:21L	-	-	-	-
10	7:51	7:59	8:17	8:31	8:40	8:54	9:12	9:20
18	P8:01	8:09	8:27	8:41	8:55	9:09	9:27	9:35
11	8:09	8:17	8:35	8:49L	-	-	-	-
19	P8:17	8:25	8:43	8:57	9:10	9:24	9:42	9:50
12	8:25	8:33	8:51	9:05L	-	-	-	-
20	P8:33	8:41	8:59	9:13	9:25	9:39	9:57	10:05
13	8:43	8:51	9:09	9:23L	-	-	-	-
14	8:58	9:06	9:24	9:38	9:40	9:54	10:12	10:20

Notes:
1. The time interval between buses at a given point is called the headway.
2. The time interval between the arrival and departure of a bus at a terminal is called its layover.
3. P indicates that a bus not already in passenger service is placed in service at the time and place shown.
4. L indicates that a bus is taken out of passenger service at the time and place shown and is sent to the garage.
5. Lv. means "leave," and Arr. means "arrive."

41. The MINIMUM headway shown between buses leaving Mack St. is _____ minutes.
    A. 8   B. 10   C. 12   D. 15

42. The ACTUAL scheduled running time from Burr St. to High St. is _____ minutes.
    A. 14   B. 32   C. 40   D. 64

43. The layover time for Bus No. 16 at Burr St. is _____ minutes.
    A. 9   B. 12   C. 15   D. 17

44. Bus No. 11 is scheduled to
    A. follow Bus No. 12 from Burr St. to Mack St., northbound
    B. leave Ace St. exactly 20 minutes after it leaves Mack St., southbound
    C. leave Burr St. for the garage after 8:49
    D. be placed in service to begin its day's run at Mack St. at 8:09

45. The time shown in the timetable for any bus to make the run from Mack St. to Burr St. and return is _____ minutes _____ the layover time at Burr St.
    A. 40; plus   B. 40; minus   C. 80; minus   D. 80; plus

46. The TOTAL number of northbound buses passing High St. between 8:00 and   46.____
    8:45 is
    A. 2   B. 3   C. 4   D. 5

47. The TOTAL number of buses which is scheduled to leave Mack St. between   47.____
    7:45 and 8:45 and is also scheduled to return to Mack St. is
    A. 4   B. 5   C. 6   D. 7

48. The MOST northerly street on this line is _____ St.   48.____
    A. Ace   B. Mack   C. High   D. Burr

49. A passenger boarding a bus at Burr St. and wishing to get to High St. as 49.____
    close as possible to 9:30 should board the bus which leaves at
    A. 8:51   B. 8:55   C. 9:06   D. 9:10

50. The number of buses which is shown in the timetable as making two   50.____
    complete roundtrips is
    A. 2   B. 3   C. 5   D. 6

KEY (CORRECT ANSWERS)

1.	D	11.	B	21.	D	31.	C	41.	A
2.	A	12.	D	22.	D	32.	C	42.	B
3.	C	13.	C	23.	C	33.	C	43.	D
4.	D	14.	C	24.	B	34.	B	44.	C
5.	D	15.	A	25.	B	35.	D	45.	D
6.	A	16.	D	26.	C	36.	A	46.	B
7.	C	17.	D	27.	B	37.	D	47.	A
8.	A	18.	B	28.	B	38.	C	48.	B
9.	B	19.	D	29.	D	39.	B	49.	B
10.	A	20.	C	30.	A	40.	D	50.	A

TEST 2

DIRECTIONS: Each question or incomplete statement is followed by several suggested answers or completions. Select the one that BEST answers the question or completes the statement. *PRINT THE LETTER OF THE CORRECT ANSWER IN THE SPACE AT THE RIGHT.*

1. The two rear wheels of a bus can turn at different speeds when necessary by means of the
    A. overdrive
    B. torque converter
    C. universal joint
    D. differential

    1.____

2. To properly perform his duties, it is LEAST important for a bus driver to
    A. know the schedule of working conditions
    B. know the Transit Authority's operating rules
    C. be able to judge speed and distance
    D. know the times he is scheduled to be at various points

    2.____

3. Manuals on driving stress the importance of allowing ample braking distance to the car ahead, the most common rule of thumb being to allow a car length for each ten miles per hour of speed.
    If the overall length of a car is 210 inches, the proper braking distance to allow at a speed of 40 miles per hour is NEAREST to _____ feet.
    A. 700   B. 500   C. 70   D. 50

    3.____

4. The safe speed on any road regardless of weather conditions is primarily a function of the ability of the vehicle operator to compensate for roadway and traffic conditions.
    The statement means MOST NEARLY that it is
    A. always safe to drive well below the posted or allowable speed
    B. permitted to drive a bus faster than the posted or allowable speed to compensate for traffic delays
    C. not safe to drive at the maximum posted or allowable speed under any weather conditions
    D. necessary for a bus operator to use his judgment to determine the safe operating speed

    4.____

5. If your watch gains 20 minutes per day and you set it to the correct time at 7:00 A.M., the correct time, to the NEAREST minute, when the watch indicates 1:00 P.M. is
    A. 12:50   B. 12:55   C. 1:05   D. 1:10

    5.____

6. The law requires that cars having four-wheel brakes must be able to stop in 30 feet from a speed of 20 miles per hour, and in 120 feet from 40 miles per hour. From these requirements and your own knowledge of automobiles in motion, it is MOST logical to conclude that
    A. the law is more lenient in regard to fast cars than slow cars
    B. when speed is doubled, the needed braking distance is multiplied by four

    6.____

C. drivers' reactions slow down greatly as speed increases
D. any 20 mile per hour increase in speed will require 90 feet more of braking distance

Questions 7-16.

DIRECTIONS: Questions 7 through 16 are to be answered on the basis of the sketch shown below. Refer to this sketch when answering these questions. The sketch shows the situation shortly after the traffic lights have changed to green for north-south traffic and red for east-west traffic.

7. Of the following stopped cars, the one which is in the generally approved position to start to enter a parking space is the one numbered
   A. 7   B. 8   C. 9   D. 11

8. It is clearly seen that the operator of Bus 1 is
   A. in error in taking up the entire bus stop
   B. not stopping, as Bus 6 will pick up the passengers
   C. driving in a westerly direction
   D. ahead of schedule

9. One car which is unquestionably illegally parked is No.
   A. 3   B. 10   C. 12   D. 25

10. The driver of Car 4 would be violating the law if he
    A. stopped at the sidewalk to pick up a passenger
    B. failed to put on his directional signal for a left turn
    C. did not blow his horn before crossing the sidewalk
    D. failed to yield the right-of-way to any vehicle on North Ave., approaching the driveway

11. The car which is in a serious moving violation of the law is No.
    A. 2   B. 4   C. 17   D. 19

12. If cars 22 and 23 are approaching the intersection and the operators of both cars are complying with the law, it is clear that Car 22
    A. is passing Car 23
    B. cannot stop before reaching the intersection
    C. is in the better position to make a left turn
    D. will continue across the intersection

13. The driver of Car 20 has signaled his intention to make a left turn into South Avenue. This diagram clearly shows that the turn
    A. was started from too far to the right
    B. is being made into a heavily traveled street
    C. is being made at an excessive speed
    D. can be made regardless of the position of Car 21

14. If only a single bus line operates on West St., it can be reasoned that MOST likely Bus
    A. 13 is scheduled to follow Bus 16   B. 16 is being taken out of service
    C. 13 is more crowded than Bus 16   D. 16 is ahead of schedule

15. It would be reasonable to infer that MOST likely
    A. no parking is allowed on West Street
    B. the department store is open for business
    C. West Street is 100 feet wide
    D. the area shown is primarily residential

16. An example of a double-parked car is No.
    A. 9   B. 10   C. 26   D. 27

17. Of the following, the GREATEST number of bus drivers will be on the day after
    A. New Year's   B. July 4th
    C. Thanksgiving   D. Christmas

18. The first aid procedure of not moving a person unless absolutely necessary is MOST important in the case of a person who has
    A. broken a finger   B. fainted
    C. collapsed from the heat D. fractured his leg

19. A bus driver making change should be on the alert for counterfeit bills. The BEST publicized means of detecting a counterfeit bill is to pay particular attention to the
    A. feel of the paper   B. clarity of the portrait
    C. width of the margin   D. size of the bill

20. The TOTAL value of 11 half-dollars, 27 quarters, 193 dimes, 108 nickels, 75 pennies is
    A. $27.70   B. $30.40   C. $37.70   D. $43.20

21. A bus operator need NOT pull over to the curb and come to a stop
    A. when signaled to do so by a policeman
    B. at a bus stop where passengers are waiting
    C. at the sound of a fire engine siren
    D. when he hears the horn of the car behind

22. The Transit Authority's reduced fare cards, which are issued to children by the school, are printed in a different color for each school month.
    If the cards used during one month were salmon color, this color would BEST be described as being
    A. pink   B. green   C. blue   D. gray

23. Bus operators have been instructed to confiscate reduced fare cards for any one of the following acts on the part of the student: (1) misbehavior, (2) vandalism, (3) passing card to another student, and (4) using card during unauthorized hours.
    On this basis, a student caught cutting the seats of a bus with a penknife would have his card lifted for reason number
    A. 1   B. 2   C. 3   D. 4

24. It is a rule that bus operators must not operate through or within established fire or police lines or over any unprotected hose of a fire department when laid down on any street unless allowed by proper authority.
    This means that a bus operator may operate his bus
    A. on the side of a street opposite a fire
    B. over a fire hose if given permission by a fireman

C. past a traffic officer as soon as the light turns green
D. across the route of a parade whenever there is a break in the parade line

25. The Transit Authority permits the posting of advertisements in buses PRIMARILY because
    A. passengers like to read the ads
    B. advertisers pay for this privilege
    C. it promotes safety
    D. it improves the interior appearances of the buses

26. Safety rules are MOST useful because they
    A. are a guide to avoid common dangers
    B. prevent carelessness
    C. fix responsibility for accidents
    D. make it unnecessary to think

27. During rush hours, passengers are requested to have the correct fare when boarding a bus MAINLY because this
    A. assures collection of all fares
    B. permits a fuller bus load
    C. results in less change being carried by the operator
    D. helps to maintain the schedule

28. Traffic regulations forbid *dangerous* or *reckless* driving.
    In the absence of special signs, an example of such *dangerous* or *reckless* driving is
    A. parking a car within 15 feet of a fire hydrant
    B. driving on a hospital street at 25 miles per hour
    C. passing a public school at noontime on a weekday at 10 miles per hour
    D. frequently changing lanes in heavy traffic at 45 miles per hour on a parkway

29. If a passenger called a bus operator improper names but took no other action, the bus operator would show good judgment by
    A. telling the passenger to keep his mouth shut
    B. acting as if the passenger were not there
    C. calling the passenger names in return
    D. driving to the nearest policeman and preferring charges

30. It is a rule that, when street obstructions leave scant clearance for buses to pass, operators must stop before passing the obstruction and never proceed until certain that clearance is sufficient and that it is safe to do so.
    This means that
    A. it is never safe to pass street obstructions
    B. every bus must stop before passing an open manhole with a fence around it
    C. the operator must stop if he must use the single narrow traffic lane between a parked truck and an open manhole
    D. the operator may always pass an obstruction as long as he stops first

31. After a passenger has tendered the bus operator a dollar bill, has paid his fare, and received change, he goes some distance toward the back of the bus and then returns to the front, stating that he was shortchanged a quarter.
The BEST action for a bus operator to take is to
    A. give him the quarter if he is sufficiently argumentative
    B. tell him to send a letter of complaint to the Mayor's complaint box
    C. inform him that change must be counted when received
    D. tell him that he must have dropped it in the bus

32. It is a rule that bus operators must not approach within 100 feet of a line of children during a school fire drill, nor interfere with, hinder, obstruct, or impede in any way whatsoever any such fire drill.
A bus operator, observing a school fire drill in progress in the next street ahead, could BEST comply with this rule by
    A. making a right turn at the corner and going around the school
    B. pulling up slowly to the person in charge of the drill
    C. stopping at the corner until the fire drill is over
    D. proceeding slowly along the opposite side of the street

33. A rule of the Transit Authority is that buses must never be moved except by operators certified as qualified, and by authorized student operators while supervised by a qualified operator.
This rule permits a bus to be moved at any time by any person
    A. who is an approved operator
    B. certified as a student operator
    C. with a chauffeur's license
    D. who knows how to operate a bus

34. When driving on a two-lane road at night, you see cars approaching from the opposite direction. You should
    A. increase your speed slightly
    B. ride partly on the shoulder of the road
    C. switch your headlights to low beam
    D. blow your horn

35. If you are the driver of a car involved in an accident in which some one is injured, you are required by law to file a report of the accident within two
    A. hours   B. days   C. weeks   D. months

36. If the rear of a car starts to skid toward the right, it is usually possible to break out of the skid by
    A. pumping the brake
    B. cutting off the ignition
    C. shifting to low gear
    D. steering toward the right

37. According to the notice for this examination, a candidate must be acceptable for bonding.
The MOST probable reason for this requirement is
    A. to encourage honesty among operators
    B. because operators handle money
    C. because it saves the cost of making an investigation
    D. to protect the city against lawsuits

38. It is MOST important for a bus driver to see that no vehicle is directly behind his bus when he is about to
    A. pull out from a bus stop
    B. pass another vehicle
    C. back up
    D. turn right

39. A vehicle is not permitted to pass a stopped school bus with red lights flashing because the flashing lights PROBABLY indicate that
    A. the school bus is about to start
    B. the school bus operator is in need of assistance
    C. an emergency vehicle is coming from the opposite direction
    D. children are crossing the road

40. The approved way to warm up a cold automobile engine is to
    A. let the engine idle before driving off
    B. add anti-freeze
    C. drive at the speed limit for a few minutes
    D. rock the car by shifting between reverse and low twice

41. In preparing to make a right turn, it is NOT necessary for you to
    A. move to the extreme right-hand lane
    B. low down
    C. give a hand or mechanical turn signal
    D. come to a full stop

42. The one of the following days this year on which bus lines in the city can expect the GREATEST number of passengers is
    A. May 30   B. June 5   C. July 4   D. December 25

43. According to the information given on the printed instructions in subway cars, a passenger wishing to recover an article believed lost in the subway should check with the
    A. change booth where he got on
    B. conductor on his train
    C. lost property office
    D. transit police office

Questions 44-50.

DIRECTIONS: Questions 44 through 50 are to be answered on the basis of the following paragraph. Refer to this paragraph in answering these questions.

DRINKING AND DRIVING

In fatal traffic accidents, a drinking driver is involved more than 30% of the time; on holiday weekends, more than 50% of the fatal accidents involve drinking drivers. Drinking to any extend reduces the judgment, self-control, and driving ability of any driver. Social drinkers, especially those who think they drive better after a drink, are a greater menace than commonly believed, and they outnumber the obviously intoxicated. Two cocktails may reduce visual acuity as much as wearing dark glasses at night. Alcohol is not a stimulant; it is classified medically as a depressant. Coffee or other stimulants will not offset the effects of alcohol; only time can eliminate alcohol from the bloodstream. It takes at least three hours to eliminate one ounce of pure alcohol from the bloodstream.

44. Alcohol is classified by doctors as a 44.____
    A. stimulant   B. sedative   C. depressant   D. medicine

45. Social drinkers 45.____
    A. never become obviously intoxicated
    B. always drink in large groups
    C. drive better after two cocktails
    D. are a greater menace than commonly believed

46. Alcohol will BEST be eliminated from the bloodstream by 46.____
    A. fresh air   B. a stimulant   C. coffee   D. time

47. More than half of the fatal accidents on holiday weekends involve _____ drivers. 47.____
    A. inexperienced   B. drinking   C. fast   D. slow

48. Drinking to any extent does NOT 48.____
    A. impair judgment   B. decrease visual acuity
    C. reduce accident potential   D. affect driving ability

49. In traffic accidents resulting in death, a drinking driver is involved 49.____
    A. about one-third of the time
    B. mainly at night
    C. more than 80% of the time
    D. practically all the time on weekends

50. After taking two alcoholic drinks, it is best NOT to drive until you have 50.____
    A. had a cup of black coffee   B. waited three hours
    C. eaten a full meal   D. taken a half-hour nap

KEY (CORRECT ANSWERS)

1. D	11. B	21. D	31. C	41. D
2. A	12. C	22. A	32. C	42. B
3. C	13. A	23. B	33. A	43. C
4. D	14. A	24. B	34. C	44. C
5. B	15. A	25. B	35. B	45. D
6. B	16. C	26. A	36. D	46. D
7. C	17. A	27. D	37. B	47. B
8. C	18. D	28. D	38. C	48. C
9. D	19. B	29. B	39. D	49. A
10. D	20. C	30. C	40. A	50. B

TEST 3

DIRECTIONS: Each question or incomplete statement is followed by several suggested answers or completions. Select the one that BEST answers the question or completes the statement. *PRINT THE LETTER OF THE CORRECT ANSWER IN THE SPACE AT THE RIGHT.*

1. There has been talk of assigning police detectives to operate taxicabs.
   The PRINCIPAL reason for making such assignments would be to
   A. protect cab patrons against robbery
   B. give detectives a chance to learn their way about the city
   C. apprehend and arrest those who are robbing cabdrivers
   D. give the police department an idea of the type of people who use cabs

2. An employee of the Transit Authority must notify the office whenever he moves and changes his address.
   The logical reason for this requirement is to
   A. enable the Authority to furnish correct information to creditors
   B. enable the Authority to contact the employee in time of need
   C. preventing the holding of two jobs
   D. help the post office, if necessary

Questions 3-14.

DIRECTIONS: Questions 3 through 14 are to be answered on the basis of the following descriptions of an automobile accident. Read the description carefully before answering these questions.

DESCRIPTION OF AUTOMOBILE ACCIDENT

Ten persons were injured, two critically, when a driverless automobile—its accelerator jammed—ran wild through the busy intersection at 8th Ave. and 42nd Street at 11:30 A.M. yesterday. The car struck a truck, overturned it, and mounted the sidewalk. Several persons were bowled over before the car was finally stopped by collision with a second truck. Police Officer Fred Black, Badge No. 82143, and said that the freak accident occurred after the car's driver, Mrs. Mary Jones, 39, of Queens, got out of the car with her daughter, Gloria, aged 3, while the engine was still running. Mr. Herbert Field, 64, of the Bronx, a passenger in the car, accidently stepped on the accelerator when he tried to get out. This caused the car to shoot forward, because the shift was in *drive*, and 5 pedestrians were thrown to the ground.

3. This accident occurred
   A. late in the morning   B. early in the morning
   C. early in the afternoon   D. late in the evening

4. The number of persons who were injured, but not critically, is
   A. 2   B. 5   C. 8   D. 10

5. The accident occurred a block away from
   A. Grand Central Terminal
   B. Times Square
   C. Union Square
   D. Pennsylvania Station

   5._____

6. The runaway car was finally stopped just AFTER it
   A. mounted the sidewalk
   B. collided with a second truck
   C. crossed the intersection
   D. bowled over several persons

   6._____

7. It can be inferred from the description that the driverless auto had
   A. power brakes
   B. power steering
   C. a turn indicator
   D. an automatic shift

   7._____

8. The number on the police officer's badge is
   A. 82314
   B. 82413
   C. 82143
   D. 82341

   8._____

9. The first name of the driver of the car is
   A. Mary
   B. Fred
   C. Gloria
   D. Herbert

   9._____

10. According to the accident description, the adult passenger lives in
    A. the Bronx, and so does the driver
    B. Queens, and so does the driver
    C. the Bronx, and the driver in Queens
    D. Queens, and the driver in the Bronx

    10._____

11. The number of pedestrians who were thrown to the ground is
    A. 2
    B. 5
    C. 7
    D. 10

    11._____

12. The person who made a statement about the runaway car was
    A. Herbert Field
    B. Mary Jones
    C. Gloria Jones
    D. Fred Black

    12._____

13. Herbert Field is older than Mary Jones by about _____ years.
    A. 25
    B. 35
    C. 51
    D. 61

    13._____

14. The car shot forward immediately after
    A. Mrs. Jones placed the shift in *drive*
    B. Mr. Field stepped on the accelerator
    C. Mrs. Jones stepped out of the car
    D. Mr. Field got out of the car

    14._____

15. Sudden stopping of a bus is to be avoided MAINLY because
    A. some injury to passengers may result
    B. some damage to the bus may result
    C. this might tie up traffic
    D. this might cause a skid

    15._____

16. To make a smooth normal stop from a speed of 30 M.P.H. on a dry roadway, the operator of a bus should apply the brakes
    A. using a pumping action, with heavy pressure on each application
    B. and maintain steady brake pressure until the bus stops
    C. and gradually increase the brake pressure as the bus comes to a stop
    D. and then partially release them as the bus comes to a stop

16.____

17. A bus operator, making his last run for the day, notices that the reading of the engine oil pressure gauge has dropped to zero when he is about 20 blocks from the end of the run.
    He would do BEST to
    A. complete the run and let the next operator report it
    B. stop and make the necessary repairs
    C. complete the run and report the condition on arrival
    D. stop the bus and telephone headquarters

17.____

18. A man can drive safely only if he has good driver training, is alert, and is
    A. less than 60 years old   B. over 25 years old
    C. familiar with the road he is on   D. familiar with traffic laws

18.____

19. A particular bus seats 34 passengers and stands half that number.
    The TOTAL passenger capacity of the bus is
    A. 41   B. 51   C. 61   D. 68

19.____

20. The fare register box on a bus shows the total number of cents collected. At the beginning of a run, the register reading of a certain box was 15750; and at the end of the run, the reading was 29750.
    The TOTAL number of $2 fares collected during the run was
    A. 83   B. 85   C. 70   D. 95

20.____

Questions 21-29.

DIRECTIONS: Questions 21 through 29 are to be answered on the basis of the sketch shown below showing the routes of the East Ave. (solid line) and the 8th St. (dotted line) buses. Refer to this sketch when answering these questions.

21. The bus route distance between the Fan St. and Gay Ave. terminals is _____ miles.
    A. 6.8   B. 7.6   C. 8.0   D. 8.8

22. A passenger MUST transfer if he is going from Gay Ave. Terminal to _____ St.
    A. Sea   B. Fan   C. 8th D. 50th

23. A bus on Key St. going toward Carp Ave. is moving
    A. north   B. east   C. west   D. south

24. Buses are NOT required to make even one left turn at the terminal at
    A. Gay Ave.   B. Fan St.   C. Rand St.   D. Sea St.

25. After discharging all passengers at the Sea St. Terminal before going around the loop, the number of right turns a bus must make to reach 8th St. is
    A. 1   B. 2   C. 5   D. 6

26. From Rand St. Terminal to Carp Ave. via 8th St., a bus travels a TOTAL distance of _____ mile(s).
    A. 0.3   B. 2.3   C. 2.8   D. 3.3

27. The street having the SHORTEST bus mileage is
    A. 50th St.   B. Gay Ave.   C. Key St.   D. 8th St.

28. One street used by buses operating in both directions is
    A. 8th St.   B. 9th St.   C. Eagle St.   D. Bee Ave.

29. The bus route distance between the Rand St. and Sea St. Terminals is _____ miles.
    A. 7.6   B. 8.1   C. 8.6   D. 9.1

Questions 30-43.

DIRECTIONS: Questions 30 through 43 are to be answered on the basis of the sketch shown on the following page. Refer to this sketch when answering these questions. The sketch shows the situation shortly after the traffic lights have changed to green for east-west traffic and red for north-south traffic.

30. After inspecting the sketch, one can see that 30.____
   A. no commercial traffic is permitted on Western St.
   B. buses operate on all street shown
   C. Eagle and Western Streets are one-way streets
   D. no trucks are permitted on Queen Ave.

31. Car Nos. 15, 16, 17, and 18 and Bus No. 3 were in the positions shown before the traffic light turned green for Belt Street.
    Cars which have all violated regulations by moving to the positions shown, even on a green light, are numbers
    A. 12, 13, 14, and 4
    B. 11, 12, 13, 4, and 5
    B. 4, 10, 11, and 12
    D. 4, 5, 6, 10, 11, and 12

32. The driver who is violating the law by leaving his lane is the driver of car number
    A. 9   B. 38   C. 44   D. 51

33. The driver who is clearly making a poor turn is the operator of vehicle number
    A. 23   B. 29   C. 38   D. 51

34. One car which is unquestionably illegally parked is number
    A. 33   B. 34   C. 49   D. 50

35. The operator of car number 41 making a right turn and seeing an eastbound pedestrian crossing Queen Avenue at about the white line should
    A. inch forward slowly, prepared to yield the right-of-way
    B. turn rapidly alongside number 43
    C. stop and wait for a green light on Queen Avenue
    D. blow his horn to hurry the pedestrian

36. The driver of car number 38 wishing to go north on Queen Avenue
    A. should blow his horn and attempt to follow car number 41
    B. must wait until the light is green for Queen Avenue
    C. should work his way over after the other cars have moved
    D. must first bring his car parallel to the curb of Western Street

37. The driver of car number 39, hearing the siren of a fire engine overtaking him from the rear, should
    A. follow car number 29 down Queen Avenue
    B. pull into the service station
    C. proceed quickly across Queen Avenue
    D. pull to the curb behind car number 40

38. The driver of the ambulance (vehicle number 26), seeing the congestion at Belt Street, would probably do BEST to
    A. turn around and find another route
    B. stop and wait until traffic opens up
    C. sound his siren and make his way through the space that opens up
    D. stop and telephone for public assistance

39. The operator of bus number 47, having found the bus stop occupied by vehicle number 48 (a U.S. Mail truck) should
    A. make the stop where he is, to take on and discharge passengers
    B. try to get the entire bus in to the curb
    C. skip the stop
    D. stop where he is but keep the doors closed until the mail truck leaves

40. Car numbers 52 and 53 have stopped in the positions shown.
It is LEAST likely that car number
    A. 52 jumped the gun
    B. 53 passed a red signal
    C. 52 was going to continue along Eagle St.
    D. 53 was going to turn into Eagle St.

41. If car number 52 had struck car number 53 and injured an occupant, the drivers could obtain the necessary forms on which to report the accident at the
    A. post office   B. library
    C. police station   D. county court house

42. One car which is unquestionably illegally parked at a public building is car number
    A. 48   B. 50   C. 54   D. 55

43. Three vehicles which are clearly in violation of the regulation against parking within feet of a crosswalk are numbers
    A. 6, 10, and 25   B. 28, 30, and 46
    C. 30, 31, and 48   D. 22, 46, and 54

44. A driver should NOT permit his engine to run for long in an enclosed area MAINLY because gasoline engine exhaust is
    A. irritating   B. explosive   C. corrosive   D. poisonous

45. Although lateness of any transit employee is undesirable, it is plain that a bus operator must make special effort to report for work on time MAINLY because
    A. he might be delayed by traffic
    B. his bus must be warmed up before leaving the garage
    C. lateness is always an indication of operator carelessness
    D. bus schedules cannot be maintained otherwise

46. Subway maps do NOT give information about the
    A. waiting time between trains
    B. location of transfer points
    C. terminals of the various lines
    D. relative positions of express stations

47. A bus requires 40 minutes to go from one terminal to another, and stops for 10 minutes at each terminal.
The MAXIMUM number of one-way trips that the bus can complete in 6 hours is
    A. 6   B. 7   C. 8   D. 9

48. The officially CORRECT hand signal for a left turn is to extend the hand and arm
    A. downward at about 45°   B. vertically downward
    C. vertically upward   D. horizontally

49. The device which permits the two rear wheels of a car to turn at different speeds is the
    A. differential
    B. universal joint
    C. torque converter
    D. overdrive

50. A bus operator reports that, while proceeding north on a certain street, the middle of the left side of his bus was hit by a truck which was making a right turn from an eastbound street.
    It follows that the bus was struck by the _____ corner of the truck.
    A. front left   B. front right   C. rear left   D. rear right

KEY (CORRECT ANSWERS)

1. C	11. B	21. D	31. B	41. C
2. B	12. D	22. A	32. A	42. C
3. A	13. A	23. C	33. B	43. B
4. C	14. B	24. C	34. C	44. D
5. B	15. A	25. A	35. A	45. D
6. B	16. D	26. D	36. C	46. A
7. D	17. D	27. C	37. D	47. B
8. C	18. D	28. A	38. C	48. D
9. A	19. B	29. B	39. A	49. A
10. C	20. C	30. C	40. D	50. A

EXAMINATION SECTION

TEST 1

DIRECTIONS: Each question or incomplete statement is followed by several suggested answers or completions. Select the one that BEST answers the question or completes the statement. *PRINT THE LETTER OF THE CORRECT ANSWER IN THE SPACE AT THE RIGHT.*

Questions 1-10.

DIRECTIONS: Questions 1 through 10, inclusive, are based on the portion of a timetable shown below. Refer to this timetable in answering these questions.

TIMETABLE – RIVERVIEW LINE - WEEKDAYS

Bus No.	NORTHBOUND				SOUTHBOUND				
	Gold St. Leave	New St. Leave	Ace St. Leave	Stone St. Arrive	Ace St. Leave	New St. Leave	Gold St. Arrive		Gold St. Leave
8	7:30	7:45	8:00	8:10	8:15	8:25	8:40	8:55	9:00
9	7:45	8:00	8:15	8:25	8:30	8:40	8:55	9:10	9:15
10	8:00	8:15	8:30	8:40	8:45	8:55	9:10	9:25	9:30
11	8:15	8:30	8:45	8:55	9:00	9:10	9:25	9:40	9:45
12	8:25	8:40	8:55	9:05	9:10	9:20	9:35	9:50	9:55
13	8:35	8:50	9:05	9:15	9:20	9:30	9:45	10:00	10:05
14	8:45	9:00	9:15	9:25	9:30	9:40	9:55	10:10	10:15
15	8:55	9:10	9:25	9:35	9:40	9:50	10:05	10:20	10:25
8	9:00	9:15	9:30	9:40	9:45	9:55	10:10	10:25	LU*
16	9:05	9:20	9:35	9:45	9:50	10:00	10:15	10:30	10:35
17	9:10	9:25	9:40	9:50	9:55	10:05	10:20	10:35	LU*
9	9:15	9:30	9:45	9:55	10:00	10:10	10:25	10:40	10:45

*LU means that the bus is taken out of passenger service at the location where LU appears.
NOTE: Assume that the arrival times at New St. and Ace St. are the same as the leaving times.

1. The length of time required for a bus to make a southbound run from Stone St. to Gold St. is _____ minutes.
   A. 40 B. 45 C. 50 D. 80

   1.____

2. The length of time that buses are scheduled to remain at Gold St. is _____ minutes.
   A. always 15 B. always 10 C. always 15 D. either 5 or 10

   2.____

3. The total length of time, including the five-minute layover at Stone St., required for one roundtrip from Gold St. to Stone St. and return is _____ minutes.
   A. 80 B. 85 C. 90 D. 125

   3.____

4. The total number of different buses listed in the portion of the timetable shown is
   A. 9 B. 10 C. 11 D. 12

   4.____

5. The number of buses for which two complete roundtrips are shown in the timetable is
   A. 1   B. 2   C. 3   D. 4

6. A person reaching New St. at 8:58 to board a southbound bus would have to wait until
   A. 9:00   B. 9:05   C. 9:10   D. 9:15

7. The average of the running times from Gold St. to New St., from New St. to Ace St., and from Ace St. to Stone St. is about _____ minutes.
   A. 12   B. 13   C. 14   D. 15

8. A passenger leaving Gold St. on the 7:30 bus is going to Stone St. to take care of some business.
   If his business takes a total of an hour and a half, he can be back at Gold St. by about
   A. 9:00   B. 9:30   C. 10:00   D. 10:30

9. From the entries in the timetable, you can infer that the location near which there is MOST likely to be a bus garage or storage yard is _____ St.
   A. Stone   B. Ace   C. New   D. Gold

10. A person reaching New St. at 8:45 to leave on a northbound bus would expect to arrive at Stone St. at
    A. 8:50   B. 9:00   C. 9:15   D. 9:30

11. A crosstown bus operate between two terminals 22 blocks apart and makes 18 stops. It takes minute to travel each block and minute at each stop, and 5 minutes are lost at traffic lights.
    The TOTAL time required to go from one terminal to the other is _____ minutes.
    A. 15   B. 17   C. 20   D. 22

12. The operator is forbidden by the rules to converse unnecessarily with passengers while driving his bus.
    A logical reason for this rule is that such conversation
    A. takes the operator's attention off his driving
    B. makes a poor impression on the other passengers
    C. tends to block the entrance to the bus
    D. may lead to an argument with undesirable consequences

13. A bus operator would NOT be taking responsible care of his employer's property if he
    A. drove faster than 20 miles per hour in cold weather
    B. opened the front doors to let a passenger off at a bus stop
    C. passed another bus while it was in a bus stop
    D. rubbed the wheels against the curb at a bus stop

14. If a bus operator has to call an ambulance for an injured person, the MOST important information he must transmit is
    A. where the ambulance is needed
    B. the name of the injured person
    C. how the accident occurred
    D. what part of the body has been injured

15. An operator entering a bus garage notices a lighting fixture that appears to be loose and in danger of falling from the ceiling.
    His BEST procedure would be to
    A. get a stepladder and tie the fixture up temporarily with cord
    B. find the switch and turn the light off
    C. tell his superior about the fixture
    D. forget it because the repairmen will find it

16. The Sunday bus timetable is generally operated in place of the regular weekday timetable when a legal holiday falls on a weekday.
    The logical reason is that passenger travel
    A. is never heavy on a holiday
    B. is heaviest on Sundays and holidays
    C. on weekdays is heavier than on holidays
    D. on holidays is generally similar to Sunday travel

17. When making change while standing at a bus stop, the bus operator should pay GREATEST attention to
    A. accuracy   B. courtesy   C. speed   D. safety

18. Courtesy to passengers is impressed on transit employees MAINLY to
    A. discourage vandalism   B. assure passenger safety
    C. speed up bus operations   D. maintain good public relations

19. It is reasonable to expect that a bus operator would be required to
    A. make minor repairs to his engine
    B. change burned out headlight lamps
    C. make written reports of his activities
    D. detail disorderly people

20. A passenger, who wishes to pay two 90-cent fares, hands the bus operator 2 dollar bills.
    If the fare box will take quarters, dimes, and nickels, the SMALLEST number of coins the passenger can be given is
    A. 10   B. 11   C. 12   D. 13

21. Employees MUST know the rules and regulations governing their jobs to
    A. please their supervisors   B. foresee emergencies
    C. avoid accidents   D. perform their duties properly

22. Bus operators are permitted to select their assignments in the order of seniority on the job.
The MOST probable reason for using this method is to
   A. discourage absenteeism
   B. give every employee the assignment he desires
   C. give new employees preference in selection
   D. reward length of service

23. The TOTAL value of an operator's change fund consisting of 7 half-dollars, 19 quarters, 169 dimes, and 105 nickels is
   A. $28.40   B. $29.40   C. $30.40   D. $31.40

24. Standard forms frequently call for entries on them to be printed.
This is done MAINLY because printing, as compared to writing, is generally
   A. more compact   B. more legal
   C. more legible   D. easier to do

25. If an angry passenger, boarding a bus at a busy stop, called the operator names because the bus was late, the operator would show BEST judgment by
   A. ignoring the name calling
   B. explaining the reason for the lateness to the passenger
   C. ejecting the passenger
   D. getting the passenger's name and address

26. On vehicles equipped with hydraulic braking, the MOST serious danger which may occur is
   A. unequal braking   B. high brake fluid pressure
   C. loss of the brake fluid   D. freezing of the brake fluid

27. On vehicles equipped with manual shifting, the practice of coasting out of gear is UNDESIRABLE because
   A. it wastes gas
   B. the driver has less control of his vehicle
   C. it causes engine damage
   D. it generally causes rear axle damage

28. If a bus operator running his bus at 25 miles per hour notices that the reading of the engine oil pressure gauge has dropped to zero, he should
   A. stop the bus
   B. speed up to 30 miles per hour
   C. drive at speeds below 20 miles per hour
   D. shift to low gear

29. It would be CORRECT to state that
   A. it is impossible to slow down on ice
   B. rain on a road increases traction
   C. chains increase skidding in snow
   D. most car skids can be avoided

30. A man CANNOT drive safely if he is
    A. driving an old car
    B. unfamiliar with traffic laws
    C. under age 25
    D. over age 60

31. It is CORRECT to state that the greater the speed of a vehicle, the
    A. easier it is to stop
    B. easier it is to turn a corner
    C. longer the tire life
    D. harder it is to control the vehicle

32. If a vehicle swerves to one side whenever a sudden stop is made, the MOST likely cause would be
    A. a defective transmission
    B. a defective rear axle
    C. uneven brakes
    D. uneven steering radius

33. The very slow driver is considered a safety menace MAINLY because
    A. he never knows where he is going
    B. he is always driving a defective vehicle
    C. other cars are constantly cutting out to pass him
    D. he may back up at any moment

34. The SAFEST procedure to follow when another car is attempting to pass you on the road is to
    A. sound your horn
    B. be prepared to slow down
    C. speed up
    D. pay no attention to him

35. The BEST procedure for a bus operator to follow at an intersection where the traffic lights are stuck in the red position for all traffic is to
    A. wait for a traffic officer
    B. proceed cautiously across the intersection when traffic permits
    C. wait for a signal maintenance man
    D. have a passenger stop opposing traffic so you can cross

36. Night driving is more dangerous than daytime driving MAINLY because
    A. road vision is reduced
    B. more drivers ignore the traffic lights
    C. more people are shopping
    D. there are fewer police cars on duty

37. As a newly appointed bus operator, your supervisor would MOST likely expect you to
    A. pay close attention to instructions
    B. complete your runs ahead of schedule time
    C. make plenty of mistakes
    D. have arguments with passengers the first few days

38. When initially warming up a bus diesel engine which is cold, the engine should be
    A. raced violently
    B. run at slightly above idling speed
    C. raced rapidly in intermittent spurts
    D. run fast enough to keep engine oil pressure at maximum indication

39. Skidding of a vehicle on a dry road would be MOST likely to occur when
    A. braking slowly
    B. accelerating slowly
    C. entering a curve at high speed
    D. accelerating rapidly going down a hill

40. The equipment which requires the HEAVIEST current from the car battery is the
    A. generator
    B. starter motor
    C. horn
    D. ignition circuit

41. The weekly pay for 8 hours a day, 5 days a week, at $7.875 an hour can be calculated as
    A. 5×8×7.785
    B. 8+×7.875
    C. 8×5×7.875
    D. 8+5×7.785

Questions 42-50.

DIRECTIONS: Questions 42 through 50, inclusive, are based on the Bus Operator Instructions given below. Read these instructions carefully before answering these questions.

BUS OPERATOR INSTRUCTIONS

When running on public streets, operators must have all running lights on during hours of darkness. Practices such as having bus interior lights burning during daylight hours or operating after dark with only half the interior lights burning are forbidden. Tampering with the light circuits and removing fuses therefrom is forbidden. Poor driving practices such as sudden starts and stops, striking curbs, spinning wheels, sliding wheels, riding with handbrake on, or operating the bus with badly overheated or knocking engine must be avoided. Tires must be frequently inspected to detect improper inflation. When adjusting inside or outside rear-view mirrors, the use of force is prohibited, since only mild pressure is required. If adjustment cannot be made by use of mild pressure, report the assembly as defective.

42. Bus operators are forbidden to
    A. inspect tires
    B. remove light fuses
    C. adjust viewing mirrors
    D. stop close to curb

43. The MOST important reason for NOT operating a bus with the engine knocking is to prevent
    A. the noise
    B. loss of power
    C. waste of gas
    D. engine damage

44. A bus operator is required to make a report with respect to
    A. sliding wheels
    B. striking curbs
    C. spinning wheels
    D. stuck mirrors

45. Running lights on a bus operating on city streets would be required before 6 P.M. on every day in the month of
    A. December
    B. April
    C. June
    D. August

46. All interior bus lights should be on when the bus   46.____
    A. is garaged for the night
    B. is being repaired
    C. is operating on public streets after dark
    D. fuses are all in place

47. Operating during daylight hours with bus interior lights on is forbidden in order 47.____
    to avoid
    A. a traffic violation   B. passenger complaints
    C. unsafe bus operation   D. unnecessary battery drain

48. Riding with the handbrake on   48.____
    A. is a good safety practice   B. is sometimes permissible
    C. does not cause brake wear   D. is forbidden

49. The bus operator is required to   49.____
    A. repair tires   B. repair defective mirror assemblies
    C. inspect tires   D. make sudden starts

50. Making frequent sudden stops would be LEAST likely to cause   50.____
    A. improper tire inflation   B. excessive brake wear
    C. passenger discomfort   D. rear end collisions

KEY (CORRECT ANSWERS)

1. A	11. C	21. D	31. D	41. C
2. A	12. A	22. D	32. C	42. B
3. B	13. D	23. C	33. C	43. D
4. B	14. A	24. C	34. B	44. D
5. B	15. C	25. A	35. B	45. A
6. C	16. D	26. C	36. A	46. C
7. B	17. A	27. B	37. A	47. D
8. D	18. D	28. A	38. B	48. D
9. D	19. C	29. D	39. C	49. C
10. C	20. A	30. B	40. B	50. A

TEST 2

DIRECTIONS: Each question or incomplete statement is followed by several suggested answers or completions. Select the one that BEST answers the question or completes the statement. *PRINT THE LETTER OF THE CORRECT ANSWER IN THE SPACE AT THE RIGHT.*

Questions 1-9.

DIRECTIONS: Questions 1 through 9, inclusive, are based on the State Motor Vehicle Bureau's Point System given below. Read this point carefully before answering these questions.

STATE MOTOR VEHICLE BUREAU'S POINT SYSTEM

The newly revised point system was effective April 1. After that date, a driver having offenses resulting in an accumulation of eight points within two years, ten points within three years, or twelve points within four years, is to be summoned for a hearing which may result in the loss of his license. Under the point system, three points are charged for speeding, two points for passing a red light or crossing a double line or failing to stop at a stop sign, one and a half points for inoperative horn or sufficient lights, and one point for improper turn or failure to notify Bureau of change of address. The Commissioner of Motor Vehicles is required to revoke a driver's license if he has three speeding violations in a period of eighteen months, or drives while intoxicated or leaves the scene of an accident or makes a false statement in his application for a driver's license. This system is necessary because studies show violations of traffic laws cause four out of five fatal accidents in the state.

1. The traffic offense which calls for license revocation if repeated three times within a period of years is
   A. passing a red light
   B. passing a stop sign
   C. crossing a double line
   D. speeding

   1.____

2. The individual who has the power to revoke a driver's license is the
   A. traffic officer
   B. motor vehicle inspector
   C. Commissioner of Motor Vehicles
   D. Traffic Commissioner

   2.____

3. Crossing a double line has a penalty of twice as many points as for
   A. making an improper turn
   B. speeding
   C. passing a red light
   D. an inoperative horn

   3.____

4. Failure of a driver to properly notify the Bureau of Motor Vehicles of a change in his address carries a penalty of_____ point(s).
   A. ½   B. 1   C. 1½   D. 2

   4.____

5. The point system is specifically designed to penalize the driver who
   A. is inexperienced
   B. repeatedly violates traffic laws
   C. is overage
   D. ignores parking violations

   5.____

6. A false statement on a driver's license application calls for a penalty of   6.____
   A. 10 points   B. 8 points
   C. license suspension   D. license revocation

7. Insufficient lights carries a penalty of _____ point(s).   7.____
   A. ½   B. 1   C. 1½   D. 2

8. A driver is summoned for a hearing if, within a period of three years, he   8.____
   accumulates _____ points.
   A. 6   B. 8   C. 10   D. 12

9. The percentage of fatal accidents caused by traffic violations is   9.____
   A. 80%   B. 70%   C. 60%   D. 50%

Questions 10-18.

DIRECTIONS: Questions 10 through 18, inclusive, are based on the bus timetable shown below. Assume layover time at Prince St. and Duke St. is negligible. Refer to this timetable when answering these questions.

TIMETABLE – REGENT PARKWAY LINE - WEEKDAYS

Bus No.	EASTBOUND				WESTBOUND			
	King St. Leave	Prince St. Leave	Duke St. Leave	Queen St. Arrive	Queen St. Leave	Duke St. Leave	Prince St. Leave	King St. Arrive
20	7:15	7:20	7:30	7:45	7:50	8:05	8:15	8:20
21	7:25	7:30	7:40	7:55	8:00	8:15	8:25	8:30
22	7:35	7:40	7:50	8:05	8:10	8:25	8:35	8:40
23	7:45	7:50	8:00	8:15	8:20	8:35	8:45	8:50
24	7:55	8:00	8:10	8:25	8:30	8:45	8:55	9:00
25	8:05	8:10	8:20	8:35	8:40	8:55	9:05	9:10
26	8:10	8:15	8:25	8:40	8:43	8:58	9:08	9:13
27	8:15	8:20	8:30	8:45	8:48	9:03	9:13	9:18
28	8:20	8:25	8:35	8:50	8:53	9:08	9:18	9:23
20	8:30	8:35	8:45	9:00	9:05	9:20	9:30	9:35
21	8:40	8:45	8:55	9:10	9:15	9:30	9:40	9:45
22	8:50	8:55	9:05	9:20	9:25	9:40	9:50	9:55

10. The total running time (omit layover) for one roundtrip from King St. to Queen St.   10.____
    and back again is _____ minutes.
    A. 70   B. 65   C. 60   D. 30

11. The LEAST time that any bus stops over at Queen St. is _____ minutes.   11.____
    A. 3   B. 5   C. 10   D. 15

12. The time required for a bus to make the Eastbound run from King St. to   12.____
    Queen St. is _____ minutes.
    A. 65   B. 60   C. 35   D. 30

13. The total number of different buses shown in the timetable is 13.____
    A. 8   B. 9   C. 10   D. 12

14. The timetable shows that the total number of buses which make two roundtrips is 14.____
    A. 1   B. 2   C. 3   D. 4

15. A person reaching Duke St. at 8:28 to leave on a Westbound bus will have to wait _____ minutes. 15.____
    A. 2   B. 5   C. 7   D. 10

16. The SHORTEST running time between any two bus stops is _____ minutes. 16.____
    A. 3   B. 5   C. 10   D. 15

17. The bus which arrives at King St. three minutes after the preceding bus is bus number 17.____
    A. 20   B. 22   C. 26   D. 28

18. Bus No. 21 is scheduled to start its second roundtrip from King St. at 18.____
    A. 9:45   B. 8:40   C. 8:30   D. 7:25

Questions 19-26.

DIRECTIONS: Questions 19 through 26, inclusive, are based on the sketch below showing the routes of the Main St. (solid line) and the Bay St. (dotted line) buses. Refer to this sketch when answering these questions.

19. The distance from the King St. Terminal to the Elm St. Terminal is _____ miles. 19.____
    A. 10   B. 9.9   C. 9.1   D. 7.6

20. A transfer is required for a passenger going from Bell St. Terminal to 20.____
    A. Bay St.   B. Dey St.   C. High St.   D. Elm St.

21. A bus running on Main St. and going from Bay St. to Elm St. is moving 21.____
    A. west   B. east   C. south   D. north

22. Buses are NOT required to make any left turns at the 22.____
    A. King St. Terminal   B. transfer point
    C. Bay St. Terminal   D. Bell St. Terminal

23. After discharging all passengers at Bell St. Terminal, the number of right 23.____
    turns required for the bus to reach Bay St. is
    A. 1   B. 2   C. 3   D. 4

24. If the average running speed of buses from King St. Terminal to the transfer 24.____
    point is 22 miles an hour, and the time for stops totals 10 minutes, then this trip
    takes _____ minutes.
    A. 25   B. 20   C. 15   D. 12

25. A bus going from Bay St. Terminal to Bell St. Terminal travels in a northerly 25.____
    direction a total distance of _____ mile(s).
    A. 0.8   B. 1.8   C. 2.7   D. 4.3

26. The street having the SHORTEST bus mileage is 26.____
    A. Bay St. B. Dey St. C. Elm St. D. King St.

27. The driver of a vehicle which injures a dog is required to report the accident 27.____
    to either the dog's owner or to
    A. a hospital   B. the S.P.C.A.
    C. the Sanitation Dept.   D. a police officer

28. Of the following, steering gear damage is MOST likely to result from 28.____
    A. sudden stops   B. fast acceleration
    C. excess lubrication   D. hitting curbs

29. At an intersection, the driver who has the preferred right-of-way is the one 29.____
    who is
    A. making a left turn   B. making a right turn
    C. proceeding straight ahead D. making a U-turn

30. If a tire blows out, it is MOST important for the driver to 30.____
    A. hold the steering wheel tightly
    B. disengage the clutch immediately
    C. shift to low gear
    D. keep his foot on the gas

31. Driving through water puddles during a rainstorm should be avoided MAINLY 31.____
    because of the danger of
    A. the wheels rusting   B. rotting the tires
    C. hitting deep holes   D. splashing the headlights

32. Axle and spring damage is MOST likely to occur on a bus which is driven 32.____
    rapidly on a roadway which
    A. has wet leaves   B. is oiled
    C. is rutted with ice   D. is sanded

33. A bus operator should never shift gears while on a railroad crossing because it may cause engine
    A. stalling
    B. knocking
    C. overheating
    D. bearing failure

34. When the wheels of a bus are struck in deep snow, the WORST thing for the bus operator to do is to
    A. back up
    B. try second gear
    C. accelerate rapidly
    D. start slowly

35. If a bus operator must leave his bus parked on a hilly street, he should park with
    A. rear wheels at least 3 inches from the curb
    B. front wheels parallel to the curb
    C. all wheels a few inches away from the curb
    D. front wheels cut into the curb

36. The MAJORITY of traffic accidents are MOST likely caused by
    A. negligence
    B. defective vehicles
    C. roadway conditions
    D. defective traffic

37. The MOST important reason for keeping traffic accident statistics is to
    A. justify law enforcement
    B. determine accident causes
    C. reduce speeding
    D. frighten pedestrians

38. Pedestrian fatalities are MOST likely to occur at
    A. crossings having traffic lights
    B. other than designated crossings
    C. railroad crossings
    D. full-stop crossings

39. Skidding on a slippery road is MOST likely to occur if the tires are
    A. new
    B. under-inflated
    C. of the cushion type
    D. over-inflated

40. Certain traffic regulations are designed to specifically protect school buses. This is MAINLY because
    A. these buses make frequent stops
    B. school children are careless pedestrians
    C. these buses travel slowly
    D. children must reach school on time

41. The driver of a truck cuts over in front of a bus, blocking further movement of the bus. He gets out of his truck and complains violently to the bus operator that the bus cut him off some distance back, forcing him to stop suddenly to avoid a collision with the bus.
    In this case, it would be BEST for the bus operator to
    A. cut the argument short by moving the obstructing truck out of the way
    B. avoid argument by saying it was unavoidable if it occurred and request the truck driver to move his truck

C. send a passenger to look for a traffic officer
D. request the passengers to verify the fact that the bus driver was not guilty of this accusation

42. A rule of the Transit Authority is that operators of buses must never accept cash fares by hand, but must request passengers to deposit their own fares in the fare box.
The MOST likely reason for this rule is to
    A. reduce the chance of money dropping to the floor of the bus
    B. register every fare through the box
    C. permit the passenger to count his change
    D. prevent distraction of the operator while he is driving the bus

42.____

43. At an intersection having no traffic light or other protection, the right-of-way belongs to
    A. the avenue traffic
    B. pedestrians attempting to cross
    C. cars attempting to turn
    D. buses crossing the intersection to make a passenger stop

43.____

44. When the bus operator sees a ball roll out into the roadway, it is MOST important for the operator to
    A. swerve the bus to avoid the ball
    B. avoid the ball by straddling the bus over it
    C. stop the bus to avoid the ball
    D. be prepared to stop

44.____

45. If a bus operator notices a vehicle which is moving erratically in the traffic ahead of his bus, then it would be BEST for the bus operator to
    A. stay behind this vehicle
    B. ask the drive to pull over to the curb
    C. be especially careful if it is necessary to pass this vehicle
    D. determine if the driver is ill

45.____

46. High school children are given special cards for reduced fare transportation on city buses when traveling to and from school.
In view of this, it is likely that
    A. these cards would be valid for use on the first day of January
    B. these cards would never be honored after 3 P.M.
    C. the card holders deposit money in the fare box
    D. these cards would not be honored before 9 A.M.

46.____

47. The right-of-way in proceeding across an intersection against a red light is NOT given to a
    A. private passenger car taking a patient from a hospital
    B. fire engine truck returning to the firehouse after a fire
    C. vehicle instructed to pass the red light by the traffic officer on duty at the intersection
    D. pedestrian guided by a seeing-eye dog

47.____

48. Operators of buses are instructed to adjust ventilators and windows to conform with weather conditions and passenger loads.
This MOST likely means that
    A. open windows are not necessary if the bus has only a few passengers
    B. for the same kind of weather, fewer windows should be opened if the bus is full
    C. all ventilators and all windows must be closed in months like September, regardless of the number of passengers
    D. for the same kind of weather, more open windows may be required when the bus is crowded

49. One of the duties of a bus operator is to issue and accept transfers for passengers using intersecting or connecting routes.
To perform this duty properly, the operator is NOT required to
    A. check the date on the transfers he accepts
    B. know the specific privileges on the transfers he issues
    C. know the specific privileges on the transfers he accepts
    D. question each passenger to whom he issues a transfer

50. The Transit Authority has specifically called to the attention of its bus operators that driving an uninsured motor vehicle results in certain penalties.
The MOST probable reason for this is to
    A. make certain a bus operator does not lose his driving license
    B. warn the operators to check the liability insurance windshield sticker required on all vehicles
    C. warn the operators who never drive a private vehicle to carry personal insurance
    D. inform the operators they should never drive a car they do not own

KEY (CORRECT ANSWERS)

1.	D	11.	A	21.	B	31.	C	41.	B
2.	C	12.	D	22.	B	32.	C	42.	B
3.	A	13.	B	23.	D	33.	A	43.	B
4.	B	14.	C	24.	A	34.	C	44.	D
5.	B	15.	C	25.	C	35.	D	45.	C
6.	D	16.	B	26.	C	36.	A	46.	C
7.	C	17.	C	27.	D	37.	B	47.	A
8.	C	18.	B	28.	D	38.	B	48.	D
9.	A	19.	B	29.	C	39.	D	49.	D
10.	C	20.	D	30.	A	40.	B	50.	A

TEST 3

DIRECTIONS: Each question or incomplete statement is followed by several suggested answers or completions. Select the one that BEST answers the question or completes the statement. *PRINT THE LETTER OF THE CORRECT ANSWER IN THE SPACE AT THE RIGHT.*

Questions 1-10.

DIRECTIONS: Questions 1 through 10, inclusive, are based on the sketch shown below. Refer to this sketch when answering these questions.

1. A car which is definitely violating a parking law is number 1.____
   A. 15 B. 22 C. 24 D. 32

2. If traffic light T turns from green to yellow for Lake St. traffic when bus No. 12 is traveling as shown, it would be BEST for the bus operator to
   A. stop where he is
   B. continue past the light
   C. back up
   D. turn left

3. If car No. 21 displaying a flashing red light is a vacant police patrol car parked in the Lake St. bus stop, then the operator of bus No. 31 normally making this stop should open his door for passengers
   A. at the bus stop, waiting until the police car moves out
   B. after pulling up past car No. 21 until rear door clears
   C. directly behind the police car
   D. right where he is

4. If traffic light S is green for Fourth Avenue traffic when bus No. 2 and car No. 4 are traveling as shown, it would be BEST for the bus operator to
   A. speed up
   B. start backing up
   C. cut in front of car No. 4
   D. slow down

5. In making the wide right turn into Lake St., the operator of bus No. 31 should
   A. consider the possibility of a car trying to pass him on his right
   B. intermittently work the directional indicator switch on and off
   C. be careful of cars making a right turn from Lake St. to Fourth Ave.
   D. have gone to the left of the light before turning

6. For bus No. 30 to make a right turn from Broad St. into Fourth Ave., traffic light U would MOST likely be
   A. green for Lake St.
   B. red for Lake St.
   C. green for Fourth Ave.
   D. red for Cross St.

7. When traffic light T turns green for Cross St., the vehicle which is in the proper position for a left turn from Cross St. to Lake St. is No.
   A. 11   B. 7   C. 6   D. 5

8. If an ambulance with its warning signal sounding is coming into Fourth Ave. from Cross St., then bus No.
   A. 14 should stop where it is
   B. 2 should turn right
   C. 2 should speed up
   D. 14 should pull in front of car No. 15 and stop

9. The total number of two-way thoroughfares shown in the sketch is
   A. 1   B. 2   C. 3   D. 4

10. If the operator of bus No. 25 on Broad St. is ready to start moving, he should wait
    A. until car No. 27 pulls in front of car No. 26
    B. for car No. 26 to move out of the way
    C. for car No. 28 to pass
    D. for traffic light U to turn green

11. When a person carrying a large package is permitted to ride a bus, it is MOST important for the bus operator to make certain that the
    A. package is not placed on an unoccupied seat
    B. passenger does not forget his package
    C. aisles and doorways are not obstructed
    D. package is securely tied and will not come apart

12. A bus operator starts out with $10.00 in change, and his fare box indicates he collects $85.50 in passenger fares. On counting his money, he finds that he has 75 one dollar bills, 10 fifty-cent pieces, 22 quarters, and 70 dimes.
    To have the CORRECT amount, the number of nickels he should have is
    A. 45   B. 50   C. 55   D. 60

13. Bus operators are required to turn in all unused transfers after completing their tour of duty.
    The MOST important reason for this rule is to
    A. provide a means for checking the bus fare totals
    B. determine if it is necessary to discontinue transfer privileges from one bus route to another
    C. prevent misuse of transfers if discarded
    D. determine if the bus operator is issuing transfers properly

14. If the operator of a bus hears two of his passengers arguing over the right to occupy a certain seat, it is BEST for the operator to
    A. decide which passenger is entitled to the seat
    B. ask both passengers to leave the bus
    C. ignore the situation unless they resort to force
    D. ask an impartial observer to settle the dispute

15. If traffic conditions permit, when passing a line of cars parked at the curb, the BEST driving procedure would be for the bus operator to drive his bus
    A. about 3 feet away from the parked cars
    B. within a few inches of the parked cars
    C. at least a car width away from these cars
    D. close to unoccupied cars and six feet away from occupied cars

16. If a bus operator is within a few bus stops from his terminal point, he would MOST likely have to request his passengers to take another bus if the
    A. rear exit door should jam in the closed position
    B. rear exit door should jam in the open position
    C. fare box should become inoperative
    D. buzzer signal system goes out of order

17. A passenger has a bus operator change a ten dollar bill, pays his fare, and seats himself. A few minutes later, he returns to the bus operator and claims his change was short by a dollar,
    The FIRST thing the bus operator should do is
    A. ask the passenger to search the floor for the missing change
    B. remind the passenger he deposited his fare in the fare box

C. give the passenger the dollar without discussing it
D. ask the passenger if he has a hole in his pocket

18. If two men ignore the bus operator's warning to stop vandalism while riding in his bus, it would be BEST for the bus operator to
    A. attract the attention of a patrolman as soon as possible
    B. ask the other passengers to leave the bus
    C. forcibly eject the trouble-makers
    D. take the names and addresses of the trouble-makers

19. It would be LEAST desirable for a bus operator whose bus is in motion to tell a passenger
    A. the location of a bus transfer point
    B. the length of time required to reach his destination
    C. to move away from the front doors
    D. why his complaint of poor service is not justified

20. When driving up a hill on a narrow roadway, passing another car is dangerous because
    A. it is difficult to make a quick stop   B. the engine will overheat
    C. steering control is lost   D. vision is limited

21. Grease on brake lining
    A. is necessary for long brake life   B. is necessary for quiet braking
    C. results in unsafe brakes   D. results in safer braking

22. Official regulations prescribe that an operator's uniform should always appear neat.
    The MOST probable reason for this requirement is that a neat uniform
    A. is easier to keep clean
    B. makes a good impression on the public
    C. attracts attention
    D. makes a better bus operator

23. Under certain roadway conditions, it is advisable to come to a stop by *pumping* the brake pedal several times instead of making a single brake application and holding it.
    Such handling of the brake is necessary when the roadway is
    A. banked   B. dark   C. bumpy   D. slippery

24. The battery in a car furnishes the energy to operate the
    A. starter   B. distributor
    C. fuel pump   D. radiator fan

25. Antifreeze is used in automobiles to
    A. heat the interior
    B. keep the windshield free of ice
    C. prevent freezing of the fuel supply
    D. keep the cooling water from freezing

26. In the average passenger car that is not over five years old, the battery is located under the 26.____
    A. driver's seat   B. dashboard   C. hood   D. chassis

27. The stock-car taxicab as compared with the older type of taxicab is definitely 27.____
    A. safer   B. shorter
    C. more comfortable   D. more expensive

28. The shape of traffic sign which means STOP is 28.____
    A. ○   B. ⬡   C. ◇   D. ▭

29. If the first day of a 30-day month falls on a Saturday, the last day of the month will fall on a 29.____
    A. Friday   B. Saturday   C. Sunday   D. Monday

Questions 30-36.

DIRECTIONS: Questions 30 through 36, inclusive, are based on the Extract of Rules for System Pick for Bus Operators given below. Read this extract carefully before answering these questions.

EXTRACT OF RULES FOR SYSTEM PICK FOR BUS OPERATORS

Operators picking an early run (one ending before 9:00 P.M. including all time allowances) on weekdays must pick an early run on Saturday and Sunday.

No operator will be allowed to pick on the extra list unless he desires to transfer to a depot where all runs, tricks, etc. have been picked.

After an operator finishes picking and the monitor has entered the operator's name for the run on the picking board, no change of run will be permitted. Erasures and other signs of mutilation will not be permitted on the picking board.

It is planned to permit about 100 men in the picking room at one time, but the time allowed for any one man to pick will not exceed five minutes. If, for any reason, you cannot attend, you may submit a preference slip or be represented by proxy.

An operator inactive because of sickness, injury, etc. for sixty days prior to his pick assignment must present a certificate from a doctor stating he may return to duty not later than two weeks after date of pick.

Your cooperation is requested. Please be on hand to pick at your designated time and leave picking room promptly when you have finished picking.

30. The rules apply to a _____ pick. 30.____
    A. Saturday and Sunday   B. depot extra
    C. weekday   D. system

31. An operator picking an early run on weekdays 31.____
    A. cannot be off on Saturdays or Sundays
    B. must submit a preference slip
    C. will be assigned to the extra list on other days
    D. must pick an early run on Saturday and Sunday

32. According to these rules, an operator 32.____
    A. will be in the picking room alone while designating his choice
    B. must wait in the picking room after making his choice until all the runs have been chosen
    C. is informed that he may pick his run at any time he wishes to on pick day
    D. may have someone else pick for him if he cannot be present on the day of the pick

33. In order to pick on the extra list, an operator must 33.____
    A. present a doctor's certificate
    B. have been inactive for sixty days
    C. appear at the picking room in person
    D. be willing to transfer to a terminal where all the runs have been picked

34. Once a bus operator picks a run and his name has been entered by the monito, he 34.____
    A. must accept the run picked as no changes will be permitted
    B. can change his mind if the choice was made by proxy
    C. may ask the monitor to erase his pick if the next man has not yet picked
    D. can swap runs with another operator but only after sixty days

35. An operator making his pick after having been out sick for three months must 35.____
    A. pick on the extra list
    B. present a doctor's certificate to the monitor
    C. wait two weeks before returning to duty
    D. pick an early run or trick

36. The rules state that 36.____
    A. only 100 men can pick in any one day
    B. cooperation is demanded and a penalty will be imposed on any operator who is uncooperative
    C. a preference slip must be signed by the monitor
    D. an operator must make his pick within 5 minutes time

Questions 37-42.

DIRECTIONS: Questions 37 through 42, inclusive, are based on the information for Operators given below. Read this information carefully before answering these questions.

INFORMATION FOR OPERATORS

In spite of caution signs and signal lights, more than 42% of all automobile accidents occur at intersections. In narrow city streets with narrow sidewalks and heavy traffic, you should approach intersections at 15 miles per hour with your foot just touching the brake pedal, in wet weather, 10 miles per hour. At rural intersections, be sure you have a clear view of the intersecting road to the right and left at least 300 feet before you reach the intersection, otherwise slow down.

At an intersection, the vehicle on your right has the right of way, if both of you reach the intersection at the same time. You have the right of way over the vehicle at your left under the same condition, but must not insist upon it if there is risk of a collision.

Do not pass another vehicle at an intersection. Stop your vehicle to allow pedestrians to cross in front of you at intersections if they have stepped off the curb. Operators must use extreme caution when approaching or turning at intersections not controlled by a signal light.

37. One of the facts given is that 37.____
    A. nearly all accidents occur at country crossroads
    B. nearly half of all accidents occur at traffic lights in cities
    C. approximately two-fifths of all accidents occur where roads or streets cross one another
    D. 42% of all accidents occur on narrow city streets

38. According to this information, if you are approaching an intersection at which 38.____
    there is no traffic light and a man has started to cross the street in front of you, you must
    A. reduce your speed to 15 miles per hour
    B. blow your horn lightly
    C. stop to allow him to cross
    D. place your foot so it just touches the brake pedal

39. At an intersection not protected by a traffic light, you should grant the right 39.____
    of way to the vehicle approaching from the
    A. right if it is 300 feet from the intersection
    B. left if it is 300 feet from the intersection
    C. opposite direction if its right turn indicator is flashing
    D. left or right if there is danger of a collision

40. In the information, it is clearly stated that an intersection should be approached 40.____
    at 15 miles per hour if you
    A. are driving on a narrow city street in heavy traffic
    B. do not see a warning sign 300 feet from the intersection
    C. do not intend to pass the vehicle ahead
    D. see a car stopped on the intersecting street waiting to cross

41. The information clearly states 41.____
    A. most city streets are narrow
    B. all city intersections should be approached at 10 miles an hour
    C. passing another vehicle at an intersection is forbidden
    D. there is a clear view of rural intersections from a distance of 300 feet

42. The type of accident referred to probably does NOT include the striking of a 42.____
    A. pedestrian by a railroad train   B. pedestrian by a passenger car
    C. bus by a taxicab   D. bus by a truck

43. The register on the fare box of a certain bus has five dials and shows the total number of cents collected. When a particular bus operator starts his tour of duty, the register reading is 08980, and at the conclusion of his tour of duty, the reading is 14560.
The total number of 90-cent fares collected during this operator's tour was
    A. 62   B. 68   C. 73   D. 77

44. Increasing use is being made today of unmarked police cars.
The PRINCIPAL reason for the use of such cars is to
    A. increase the city's revenue from traffic tickets
    B. enforce the regulation against hitchhikers
    C. prevent accidents by stopping traffic violators
    D. man them with detectives instead of uniformed policemen

45. The operator of the car ahead going at about the speed limit extends his hand and arm in a straight line at about 45 degrees upward.
Since this is not one of the standard hand signals, your SAFEST move is to
    A. swing out and pass him immediately to avoid any more confusion
    B. remain behind prepared for any move on his part until the situation is clarified
    C. pull up alongside and tell him to signal properly
    D. blow your horn until he gives a correct signal

46. Colored lights in the shape of arrows are used to help control traffic at certain intersections.
When a driver approaches a signal consisting of a green light, a green arrow pointing to the right, and a red arrow pointing to the left, he knows that he is permitted to go straight ahead
    A. if in the right-hand lane only
    B. or make a right turn, but not a left turn
    C. only if there is no cross traffic from the right
    D. but watch out for merging traffic from the left

47. The meaning conveyed by a *Yield Right-of-Way* sign is that drivers must
    A. come to a complete stop before passing the sign
    B. grant the right-of-way to oncoming traffic making a left turn
    C. grant the right-of-way to cars on the intersecting street
    D. grant the right-of-way to pedestrians

48. The law requires that cars having four-wheel brakes must be able to stop in 30 feet from a speed of 20 miles per hour, and in 120 feet from 40 miles per hour.
From these requirements and your own knowledge of automobiles in motion, it is MOST logical to conclude that
    A. the law is more lenient in regard to fast cars than slow ones
    B. when speed is doubled, the needed braking distance is multiplied by four
    C. drivers' reactions slow down greatly as speed increases
    D. any 20 mile per hour increase in speed will require 90 feet more of braking distance

49. One of the rules governing bus operators states that *They must not use omnibuses to push other omnibuses or vehicles unless ordered by a member of the supervisory force.*
    According to this rule, if a taxicab driver asks the operator of an empty bus to give him a push to get started, the operator should
    A. tell the taxicab driver it is against the rules, and go on
    B. do so if there is a patrolman nearby
    C. telephone headquarters to get permission
    D. tell the taxicab driver to ask the operator of a private car

50. A particular bus has twelve cross seats holding two passengers each, plus rear and longitudinal seats holding a total of 14 additional passengers.
    If the number of standees permitted on a bus is one-half the number of seated passengers, the total passenger capacity of this bus is
    A. 26   B. 38   C. 39   D. 57

KEY (CORRECT ANSWERS)

1. A	11. C	21. C	31. D	41. C
2. B	12. D	22. B	32. D	42. A
3. B	13. C	23. D	33. D	43. A
4. D	14. C	24. A	34. A	44. C
5. A	15. A	25. D	35. B	45. B
6. B	16. B	26. C	36. D	46. B
7. D	17. B	27. B	37. C	47. C
8. D	18. A	28. B	38. C	48. B
9. A	19. D	29. C	39. D	49. A
10. C	20. D	30. D	40. A	50. D

ARITHMETICAL REASONING
EXAMINATION SECTION
TEST 1

DIRECTIONS: Each question or incomplete statement is followed by several suggested answers or completions. Select the one that BEST answers the question or completes the Statement. *PRINT THE LETTER OF THE CORRECT ANSWER IN THE SPACE AT THE RIGHT.*

1. The weekly pay for 8 hours a day, 5 days a week, at $16.8750 an hour can be calculated as

   A. 5 x 8 x 16.8570
   B. 8 + 5 x 16.8750
   C. 8 x 5 x 16.8750
   D. 8 + 5 x 16.8570

   1.____

2. A bus operator starts out with $10.00 in change, and his fare box indicates he collects $85.50 in passenger fares. On counting his money, he finds he has 75 one dollar bills, 10 fifty cent pieces, 22 quarters, and 70 dimes.
   To have the CORRECT amount, the number of nickels he should have is

   A. 45   B. 50   C. 55   D. 60

   2.____

3. The register on the fare box of a certain bus has 5 dials and shows the total number of cents collected. When a particular bus operator starts his tour of duty, the register reading is 08980, and at the conclusion of his tour of duty the reading is 14540.
   The TOTAL number of 20-cent fares collected during this operator's tour was

   A. 278   B. 598   C. 783   D. 969

   3.____

4. A particular bus has 12 cross seats holding two passengers each, plus rear and longitudinal seats holding a total of 14 additional passengers.
   If the number of standees permitted on a bus is one-half the number of seated passengers, the TOTAL passenger capacity of this bus is

   A. 26   B. 38   C. 39   D. 57

   4.____

5. A crosstown bus operates between two terminals 22 blocks apart and makes 18 stops. It takes half a minute to travel each block and a quarter of a minute at each stop, and 5 minutes are lost at traffic lights.
   The TOTAL time required to go from one terminal to the other is _____ minutes.

   A. 15 1/2   B. 17 1/2   C. 20 1/2   D. 22 1/2

   5.____

6. The TOTAL value of an operator's change fund consisting of 7 half-dollars, 19 quarters, 169 dimes, and 105 nickels is

   A. $28.40   B. $29.40   C. $30.40   D. $31.40

   6.____

7. If it takes a bus 30 seconds to pass two checkpoints that are 500 feet apart, then the speed of the bus is APPROXIMATELY _____ m.p.h.

   A. 10.1   B. 11.4   C. 12.7   D. 14.2

   7.____

8. If the length of a particular bus route is 8.6 miles and the average speed of a bus on this route is 7.5 miles per hour, then the ONE-WAY running time for a bus is _____ minutes.

   A. 52.3 B. 64.5 C. 68.8 D. 75.6

9. If your watch gains 20 minutes per day and you set it to the correct time at 7:00 A.M., the correct time, to the NEAREST minute, when the watch indicates 1:00 P.M. is

   A. 12:50 B. 12:56 C. 1:05 D. 1:10

10. A particular bus seats 34 passengers and stands half that number.
    The TOTAL passenger capacity of the bus is

    A. 41 B. 51 C. 61 D. 68

11. The fare register box on a bus shows the total number of cents collected. At the beginning of a run, the register reading of a certain box was 15750 and at the end of the run the reading was 17150.
    The TOTAL number of $1.00 fares collected during the run was

    A. 16 B. 17 C. 14 D. 19

12. Manuals on driving stress the importance of allowing ample braking distance to the car ahead, the most common rule of thumb being to allow a car length for each ten miles per hour of speed.
    If the overall length of a car is 210 inches, the proper braking distance to allow at a speed of 40 miles per hour is NEAREST to _____ feet.

    A. 700 B. 500 C. 70 D. 50

13. A bus requires 40 minutes to go from one terminal to another and stops for 10 minutes at each terminal. The MAXIMUM number of one-way trips that the bus can complete in 6 hours is

    A. 6 B. 7 C. 8 D. 9

Questions 14-21.

DIRECTIONS: Questions 14 through 21 in Column I are questions of simple arithmetic, each of which has one of the answers listed in Column II. For each item in Column I, select the CORRECT answer from Column II.

COLUMN I	COLUMN II
14. 229 times 9	A. 1,383
15. 11,064 divided by 8	B. 1,752
16. 1,384 plus 368	C. 2,061
17. 3,021 minus 447 minus 386	D. 2,682
18. 149 times 3 times 6	E. 2,188
19. 727 plus 17 plus 639	

20. 2,881 minus 693   20.____

21. 43,281 divided by 3 divided by 7   21.____

Questions 22-25.

DIRECTIONS: Questions 22 through 25 in Column I are questions of simple arithmetic, each of which has one of the answers listed in Column II. For each item in Column I, select the CORRECT answer from Column II.

COLUMN I	COLUMN II	
22. 198 times 3 times 4	A. 1,267	22.____
23. 837 plus 18 plus 412	B. 2,376	23.____
24. 8,869 divided by 7	C. 1,944	24.____
25. 2,693 minus 509	D. 1,867	25.____
	E. 2,184	
	F. 2,076	

KEY (CORRECT ANSWERS)

1. C   11. C
2. D   12. C
3. A   13. B
4. D   14. C
5. C   15. A

6. C   16. B
7. B   17. E
8. C   18. D
9. B   19. A
10. B   20. E

21. C
22. B
23. A
24. A
25. E

4 (#1)

SOLUTIONS TO PROBLEMS

1. Weekly pay = 5 x 8 x 16.8750
2. $10.00 + $85.50 - ($75+$5+5.50+$7) = $3 = 60 nickels
3. 14,540 - 08980 = 05560, and 5560 ÷ 20 = 278
4. Number of people sitting = (12)(2) + 14 = 38. Number of people on bus = 38 + (1/2)(38) = 57
5. Total time = (22)(1/2) + (18)(1/4) + 5 = 20.5 minutes
6. (7)(.50) + (19)(.25) + (169)(.10) + (105)(.05) = $30.40
7. 500 ft in 30 sec = 16 2/3 ft per sec. Since 60 mph = 88 ft per sec, the bus' speed = (60)(16 2/3/88) 11.4 mph
8. Let x = number of minutes. Then, 7.5/60 = 8.6/x. Solving, x = 68.8
9. If the watch gains 20 mins. in 24 hrs., it gains 5/6 min. or 50 seconds in 1 hour. In 6 hours, from 7:00 AM to 1:00 PM, it gains 5 mins: (6 x 5/6). When the watch indicates 1:00 PM, the correct time is 12:55 PM.
10. Passenger capacity = 34 + (1/2)(34) = 51
11. 17150 - 15750 = 1400, so 1400 cents = 14 $1 fares
12. (210 in.)(40/10) = 840 in. = 70 ft.
13. 6 hrs. ÷ 5/6 hr. = 7.2, so 7 trips would be the maximum number.
14. (229)(9) = 2061
15. 11,064 ÷ 8 = 1383
16. 1384 + 368 = 1752
17. 3021 - 447 - 386 = 2188
18. (149)(3)(6) = 2682
19. 727 + 17 + 639 = 1383
20. 2881 - 693 = 2188
21. 43,281 ÷ 3 ÷ 7 = 2061
22. (198)(3)(4) = 2376
23. 837 + 18 + 412 = 1267
24. 8869 ÷ 7 = 1267
25. 2693 - 509 = 2184

TEST 2

DIRECTIONS: Each question or incomplete statement is followed by several suggested answers or completions. Select the one that BEST answers the question or completes the statement. *PRINT THE LETTER OF THE CORRECT ANSWER IN THE SPACE AT THE RIGHT.*

1. A bus depot took in $308,645.00 during a 3-month period. During the following 3-month period, the revenue decreased 17%.
   The revenue for the second 3-month period was MOST NEARLY

   A. $333,890.00   B. $283,400.00
   C. $256,175.00   D. $238,655.00

   1._____

2. A surface line dispatcher desires to check the speed of a certain bus.
   If he times the bus as traveling 220 feet in 4.9 seconds, then the bus is traveling at APPROXIMATELY_____ m.p.h.

   A. 20   B. 30   C. 36   D. 44

   2._____

3. If the thickness of material worn from a bus brake lining is approximately .20 inch for every 3,000 miles of wheel travel, then the number of miles the wheel will have traveled to reduce the thickness from .75 inch to .25 inch is

   A. 3,750   B. 6,000   C. 7,500   D. 11,250

   3._____

4. A dispatcher desires to check the speed of a certain 40-foot bus.
   If he times the bus as passing him in 1.5 seconds, then the bus is traveling at APPROXIMATELY_____ m.p.h.

   A. 15   B. 18   C. 22   D. 27

   4._____

5. The number of feet required to bring a bus traveling at 30 m.p.h. to a stop at a braking rate of 3 miles per hour per second is NEAREST to _____ feet.

   A. 180   B. 200   C. 220   D. 240

   5._____

6. A bus leaves one time point at 10:35 and arrives at the next time point at 11:00.
   If the distance between the time points is 3 miles, the average speed of the bus, in m.p.h., was MOST NEARLY

   A. 6   B. 6 1/2   C. 7   D. 7 1/2

   6._____

7. Eighty percent of the 300 operators in your depot are married, and 50% of all operators are under 35 years of age.
   The MINIMUM number of married operators in this lower age group is

   A. 60   B. 90   C. 150   D. 240

   7._____

8. A bus maintained a speed of 5 m.p.h. for one-third of its route, 10 m.p.h. for the second third, and 15 m.p.h. for the final third.
   The AVERAGE speed for the entire route was CLOSEST to _____ m.p.h.

   A. 8   B. 9   C. 10   D. 11

   8._____

89

9. During the month of August, approximately 900,000 more passengers used the surface lines than during the same month the year before. This was an increase of about 3%. The total number of passengers who used this surface transportation system during August was NEAREST to

   A. 3,000,000
   B. 3,900,000
   C. 29,000,000
   D. 31,000,000

10. Assume that there are 300 bus operators at terminal A. Terminal B has 85% as many bus operators as terminal A, and terminal C has 90% as many bus operators as terminal B. The number of operators assigned to terminal C is NEAREST to

    A. 230   B. 245   C. 255   D. 270

11. A bus leaves the terminal on time at 11:48 A.M. and after one roundtrip returns 11 minutes late at 1:06 P.M. It leaves again on time at 1:12 P.M.
    If the scheduled recovery time at both ends of the line is the same, the scheduled terminal-to-terminal running time, in minutes, is

    A. 25   B. 33   C. 42   D. 50

12. A bus line had a schedule headway of 6 minutes. Run #7 left the near terminal at 10:45 A.M. and shortly thereafter had to be taken out of service on account of engine trouble. Its passengers were picked up by its follower, run #8. The delay caused run #8 to arrive at the far terminal 6 minutes late.
    If the time of arrival of run #8 was 11:53 A.M., then the scheduled running time for the trip was _____ minutes.

    A. 44   B. 56   C. 68   D. 96

13. If a fuel storage tank contains 11,200 gallons of fuel when it is 85% full, its MAXIMUM capacity, in gallons, is CLOSEST to

    A. 9,589   B. 13,175   C. 13,274   D. 14,107

14. Assume that a total of 345 people are employed at a certain location.
    If 2/5 of these people report to work at 7:00 A.M. and another 1/5 at 8:00 A.M., then the number of people that have NOT yet reported to work is

    A. 73   B. 138   C. 154   D. 199

15. Assume that a bus consumes an average of 8 gallons of fuel per hour and that each gallon of fuel weighs 7 1/4 pounds.
    In a 6 hour period, the amount of fuel used, in pounds, is

    A. 108   B. 232   C. 348   D. 399

16. The opening Metrocard reading on a daily register is 1,152, and the last Metrocard closing reading is 1,463. The opening cash reading is 12,015, and the last cash closing reading is 24,345. (Reading increases by 30 for each fare.) The total number of revenue-paying passengers that this bus carried on this day is CLOSEST to

    A. 722   B. 1,112   C. 1,463   D. 12,330

17. If it takes a bus 30 seconds to pass two checkpoints that are 500 feet apart, then the speed of the bus is APPROXIMATELY _____ m.p.h.

   A. 10.1   B. 11.4   C. 12.7   D. 14.2

17._____

18. If the length of a particular bus route is 8.6 miles and the average speed of a bus on this route is 7.5 miles per hour, then the one-way running time for a bus is _____ minutes.

   A. 52.3   B. 64.5   C. 68.8   D. 75.6

18._____

19. A certain bus route is five miles long. The schedule speed for half of the route is 6 m.p.h., and for the other half of the route it is 15 m.p.h.
    The AVERAGE schedule speed for the entire route

   A. is between 6 m.p.h. and 10.5 m.p.h.
   B. is exactly 10.5 m.p.h.
   C. is between 10.5 m.p.h. and 15 m.p.h.
   D. cannot be calculated without knowing running time for each half of the route

19._____

20. A regular tour of duty for an operator requires him to report at 5:50 A.M., leave on his first run at 6:05 A.M., swing from 10:30 A.M. to 2:00 P.M., complete his last run at 5:10 P.M., and clear/at 5:20 P.M. (Notpaid ..for swing time.) The normal pay for this tour is at the operator's regular rate for _____ hours, _____ minutes.

   A. 9; 30   B. 9; 45   C. 10; 15   D. 11; 30

20._____

21. An employee who has a wristwatch which gains 30 minutes per day sets it to the correct time at 6:00 A.M.
    When the watch indicates 12:00 Noon, the CORRECT time, to the nearest minute, is

   A. 11:46   B. 11:53   C. 12:07   D. 12:14

21._____

22. The one-way running time on a bus route is 1 hour and 6 minutes, and the average speed of a bus on this route is 14 m. p.h.
    What is the length, in miles, of this route?

   A. 13.5   B. 14.0   C. 14.4   D. 15.4

22._____

23. A bus consumes 45 gallons of fuel after having traveled a distance of 328 miles.
    The number of miles per gallon of fuel that this bus gets, based on this information, is CLOSEST to

   A. 6.8   B. 7.3   C. 7.8   D. 8.3

23._____

24. A bus operator with a weekday run whose hourly rate of pay is $12.60 normally reports for work at 7:30 A.M. and clears at 3:00 P.M.(On report days he works until 4 P.M.) What is his gross pay for a day on which he is required to write an accident report at the end of his run?

   A. $107.10   B. $108.90   C. $113.40   D. $115.60

24._____

25. A passenger count was made at a certain terminal between 8 A.M. and 9 A.M., and it was noted that eight buses were loaded with the following number of passengers: 34, 52, 29, 63, 19, 17, 56, and 42, respectively.
The TOTAL number of passengers boarding these eight buses was

    A. 302   B. 312   C. 313   D. 412

25.____

KEY (CORRECT ANSWERS)

1. C
2. B
3. C
4. B
5. C

6. C
7. B
8. A
9. D
10. C

11. A
12. B
13. B
14. B
15. C

16. A
17. B
18. C
19. A
20. B

21. B
22. D
23. B
24. A
25. B

SOLUTIONS TO PROBLEMS

1. ($308,645)(.83) ≈ $256,175

2. 220 ft. in 4.9 sec ≈ 45 ft. per sec. Since 60 mph means 88 ft.per sec., the bus is moving at (60)(45/88) ≈ 30 mph

3. .75 - .25 = .50. Then, (3000) (.50/.20) = 7500 miles

4. 40 ft. in 1.5 sec. = 26 2/6 ft. per sec. Thus, the bus is moving at (60)(26 2/3/88) ≈ 18 mph

5. Initial speed is 30 mph = 44 ft. per sec. Final speed (when fully stopped) is 0 ft. per sec. Average speed = 22 ft. per sec. Distance = (average speed)(time) = (22)(10 sec.) = 220 ft.

6. 3 miles in 25 min. means (3)(60/25) = 7.2 ≈ 7 mph

7. Let x = minimum number of married operators under 35 years old. Then, 240-x = number of married operators over 35 years old, and 150-x = number of unmarried operators under 35 years old. Since there are probably operators who are neither married nor under 35 years old, (240-x) + (x) + (150-x) ≤ 300. Solving, x ≥ 90.

8. 5 mph= 1/3; 10 mph= 1/3; 15 mph= 1/3. 5 + 10 + 15= 30. 30 divided by 3= 10 mph average speed.

9. 900,000 ÷ .03 = 30,000,000. Then, 30,000,000 + 900,000 = 30,900,000 ≈ 31,000,000 passengers in August.

10. Terminal B has (300X.85) = 255 operators, so terminal C has (255)(.90) ≈ 230 operators.

11. The scheduled running time for a roundtrip from 11:48 AM to 12:55 PM is 67 minutes. Since the recovery time is 17 minutes (12:55 PM - 1:12 PM), and recovery time must only be deducted once from the running time for a roundtrip, the scheduled running time from terminal to terminal is $\frac{67-17}{2} = \frac{50}{2} = 25$

12. From 10:45 AM to 11:53 AM is 68 minutes. Then, 68 - 6 - 6 = 56 minutes for the scheduled running time.

13. 11,200 ÷ .85 ≈ 13,176, closest to 13,175 gallons

14. (1 - 2/5 - 1/5)(345) = 138 people

15. (6)(8)(7 1/4) = 348 pounds of fuel

16. Number of people paying by Metrocard = 1463 - 1152 = 311 Number of people paying by cash = (24,345-12,015) ÷ 30 = 411 Total of individuals paying revenue = 722

17. 500 ft. in 30 sec. means 16 2/3 ft. per sec. Then, the speed of the bus = (60)(16 2/3 ÷ 88) ≈ 11.4 mph

18. 8.6 ÷ 7.5 = 1.14$\overline{6}$ hrs. = 68.8 min.

19. Times for each half are $\frac{2.5}{6} = .41\overline{6}$ hrs. and $\frac{2.5}{15} = .1\overline{6}$ min. Average speed = 5 ÷ (.41$\overline{6}$ + .1$\overline{6}$) ≈ 8.6 mph; thus, it is between 6 mph and 10.5 mph.

20. His tour extends from 5:50 AM to 5:20 PM, for a total period of 11 1/2 hours, less swing time from 10:30 AM to 2:00 PM, which is 3 1/2 hours. 11 1/2 - 3 1/2 = 8 hours

21. 30 min/1440 min = $.0208\overline{3}$ gain. Thus, 6 hrs. on the watch indicates $6 \div 1.0208\overline{3} \approx 5.88$ hrs. hrs. ≈ 5 hrs. 53 min. in actual time. The actual time is 11:53 AM.

22. Let x = miles on this route. Then, $\dfrac{14}{x} = \dfrac{1 \text{ hr.}}{1.10 \text{ hrs.}}$ Solving, x = 15.4

23. $328 \div 45 \approx 7.3$ miles per gallon

24. 7:30 AM to 4:00 PM = 8 1/2 hrs. Then, ($12.60)(8.5) = $107.10

25. 34 + 52 + 29 + 63 + 19 + 17 + 56 + 42 = 312 passengers

TEST 3

DIRECTIONS: Each question or incomplete statement is followed by several suggested answers or completions. Select the one that BEST answers the question or completes the statement. *PRINT THE LETTER OF THE CORRECT ANSWER IN THE SPACE AT THE RIGHT.*

1. The total automobile traffic of a bridge increased from 33,000 to 37,000. This represents an increase of APPROXIMATELY

   A. 8%   B. 12%   C. 16%   D. 20%

   1.____

2. Eighty percent of the vessels passing under a certain bridge are tugboats. If 105 vessels pass under this bridge daily, the number of tugboats passing under the bridge daily is

   A. 80   B. 84   C. 88   D. 92

   2.____

3. A certain shelf can safely hold 140 pounds. On the shelf is a 45 pound carton of nuts and bolts, a 52 pound carton of assorted hardware, and two containers of lead paint weighing 27 lbs. each.
   The shelf

   A. is overloaded by 16 lbs.
   B. can safely hold an additional 16 lbs.
   C. is overloaded by 11 lbs.
   D. can safely hold an additional 11 lbs.

   3.____

4. Of the following decimals, the one which has the same value as 3/8 is

   A. 0.125   B. 0.266   C. 0.333   D. 0.375

   4.____

5. If an iron bar 6'6 1/8" long is cut in half, the length of each piece will then be MOST NEARLY

   A. 3'3 1/16"   B. 3'3 1/8"
   C. 3'6 1/8"   D. 3'6 1/4"

   5.____

6. The amount of liquid that can be stored in 72 one-quart cans is _____ gallons.

   A. 9   B. 18   C. 24   D. 36

   6.____

7. Suppose that an officer carried two packages, one weighing 73 pounds and the other weighing 41 pounds 3 ounces.
   The DIFFERENCE between the weights of the two packages was _____ pounds _____ ounces.

   A. 31; 5   B. 31; 13   C. 32; 6   D. 32; 12

   7.____

8. Suppose that the toll money collected at a bridge during March of last year was $153,696.
   If the toll money collected at this bridge in April was 3% higher than in March, then the April total was MOST NEARLY

   A. $149,085   B. $158,307   C. $167,431   D. $200,075

   8.____

2 (#3)

9. Suppose that 10% more vehicles crossed a certain bridge on Friday than on the previous day.
   If 18,100 cars, 1,290 trucks, and 130 buses used the bridge on Thursday, how many cars, trucks, and buses crossed the bridge on Friday?

   A. 17,568   B. 18,144   C. 19,520   D. 21,472

10. The maximum height allowed for vehicles using a particular bridge under normal conditions is 13 feet 6 inches.
    If a vehicle is 15 feet 5 inches tall, by exactly what amount does the vehicle EXCEED the maximum height limit for this bridge?
    _____ foot(feet) _____ inch(es).

    A. 1; 9   B. 1; 11   C. 2; 1   D. 2; 3

11. The number of cars, trucks, and buses using two different toll lanes on a certain day was as follows:

	Lane 1	Lane 2
Cars	994	1,086
Trucks	113	51
Buses	31	16

    A comparison of these two lanes would show that the TOTAL number of cars, trucks, and buses using Lane 1 on that day was _____ than the total at Lane 2.

    A. 15 fewer   B. 25 fewer   C. 15 more   D. 25 more

12. A certain officer was assigned to collect tolls for two hours. The officer was given $80 in various bills and $150 in quarters so that he could make change. He placed this money in a drawer in the toll booth. At the end of the two hours of toll collecting, the officer had a total of $1,375.75 in the drawer.
    The percent of this total which represents the tolls collected is MOST NEARLY

    A. 15%   B. 63%   C. 78%   D. 83%

13. The number of vehicles using a particular lane each hour during a 6-hour period varied as follows: 134, 210, 213, 234, 111, and 118.
    The AVERAGE number of vehicles per hour using the toll lane during this period was

    A. 150   B. 160   C. 170   D. 180

14. Assume that you have been assigned to a shift which begins at 2:00 P.M., and you want to arrive 10 minutes before the shift begins. If you average 28 miles per hour while driving to work and must travel 21 miles, at exactly what time should you start driving to work?

    A. 12:30 P.M.   B. 12:40 P.M.
    C. 1:05 P.M.   D. 1:15 P.M.

15. A rectangular storage room is 15 ft. by 16 ft., and the ceiling height is 10 feet.
    The volume of this room, in cubic feet, is

    A. 2,200   B. 2,300   C. 2,400   D. 2,500

16. One-quarter of the 168 light bulbs on a certain bridge are replaced during the year. If these bulbs cost the city 21 cents each, the yearly cost of replacing the bulbs is

    A. $8.40   B. $8.82   C. $8.86   D. $8.92

16._____

17. If 14,229 is divided by 17, the answer is

    A. 737   B. 747   C. 837   D. 847

17._____

18. A worker receives $171.50 per day.
    In 15 working days, his TOTAL earnings should be

    A. $2,560.50   B. $2,562.50
    C. $2,570.50   D. $2,572.50

18._____

19. If an Assistant Bridge Operator earns $24,500 in the first six months of a year and receives a 10% raise in salary for the next six months of the same year, his total earnings for the year will be

    A. $50,900   B. $51,450   C. $52,750   D. $53,950

19._____

20. The area of the metal plate shown at the right, minus the hole area, is MOST NEARLY _____ square inches.
    A. 8.5
    B. 8.9
    C. 9.4
    D. 10.1

20._____

21. The percentage of the tank shown at the right that is filled with water is MOST NEARLY
    A. 33
    B. 35
    C. 37
    D. 39

21._____

22. Assume that a sump pit measures 10 feet long, 10 feet wide, and 12 feet deep. If each cubic foot of water is equal to 7.5 gallons, the amount of water in the sump when half full will be MOST NEARLY _____ gallons.

    A. 120   B. 1,200   C. 4,500   D. 9,000

22._____

23. If the water in a sump pit is 10 feet deep, the pressure at the bottom of the pit, in lbs. per sq. in., exerted by the water is MOST NEARLY (assuming water weighs 62.4 lbs./cu. ft.)

    A. 4.3   B. 52   C. 62.4   D. 624

23._____

24. If part of a walkway measuring 9 feet by 20 feet is to be replaced by concrete 6 inches thick, the cubic yards of concrete needed is MOST NEARLY

    A. 1 1/2   B. 3 1/2   C. 42   D. 90

24._____

25. A new bridge spanning a river is expected to carry 60,000 cars a day on a rainy day and 80,000 cars a day on other kinds of days.
If there is a $1 toll and one chance in four of a rainy day, the expected value of a day's revenue is

    A. $35,000   B. $75,000   C. $95,000   D. $140,000

25. ____

KEY (CORRECT ANSWERS)

1.	B	11.	A
2.	B	12.	D
3.	C	13.	C
4.	D	14.	C
5.	A	15.	C
6.	B	16.	B
7.	B	17.	C
8.	B	18.	D
9.	D	19.	B
10.	B	20.	B

21. D
22. C
23. A
24. B
25. B

SOLUTIONS TO PROBLEMS

1. $4000 \div 33{,}000 \approx 12\%$
2. $(105)(.80) = 84$ tugboats
3. $140 - 45 - 52 - (2)(27) = -11$, so the shelf is overloaded by 11 lbs.
4. $3/8 = .375$
5. $(6'6\frac{1}{8}") \div 2 = 3'3\frac{1}{16}"$
6. Since 4 quarts = 1 gallon, 72 quarts = 18 gallons
7. 73 lbs. - 41 lbs. 3 oz. = 31 lbs. 13 oz.
8. $(\$153{,}696)(1.03) = \$158{,}307$
9. $(18{,}100 + 1{,}290 + 130 \times 1.10) = 21{,}472$ vehicles crossed the bridge on Friday.
10. 15 ft. 5 in. - 13 ft. 6 in. = 1 ft. 11 in.
11. Lane 1 had 1138 vehicles, whereas lane 2 had 1153 vehicles. Lane 1 had 15 fewer vehicles than lane 2.
12. Tolls collected = $\$1375.75 - \$230 = \$1145.75$. Then, $\$1145.75 \div \$1375.75 \approx 83\%$
13. $(134+210+213+234+111+118) \div 6 = 170$ vehicles
14. $21/28 = .75$ hr. Then, 1:50 PM - .75 hr. = 1:05 PM
15. Volume = $(15')(16')(10') = 2400$ cu.ft.
16. Cost = $(.21)(168)(1/4) = \$8.82$
17. $14{,}229 \div 17 = 837$
18. Total earnings = $(\$171.50)(15) = \$2572.50$
19. Total earnings = $\$24{,}500 + (1.10)(\$24{,}500) = \$51{,}450$
20. $(4)(3) - (\pi)(1)^2 = 8.9$ sq.in.
21. $\dfrac{7"}{18"} \approx 39\%$
22. Half the volume = $(1/2)(10)(10)(12) = 600$ cu.ft.
    Then, $(600)(7.5) = 4500$ gallons
23. Since 1728 cu.in. = 1 cu.ft., 62.4 lbs./cu.ft. = $0.36\overline{1}$ lbs./cu.in. With a depth of 10 ft. or 120 in., pressure = $(.0361 \times 120) \approx 4.3$ lbs./in.^{2}
24. $(9')(20')(1/2') = 90$ cu.ft. $= 90/27 = 3\,1/3$ or about $3\,1/2$ cu.yds.
25. $(\$80{,}000)(.75) + (\$60{,}000)(.25) = \$75{,}000$

BASIC FUNDAMENTALS OF DRIVING

CONTENTS

		Page
I.	WHAT TO WATCH OUT FOR IN YOUR VEHICLE	1
	A. Brakes	1
	B. Tires	1
	C. Steering	1
	D. Lights	1
	E. Windshield	1
	F. Wipers	2
	G. Mirrors	2
	H. Wheel Alignment	2
II.	RULES OF THE ROAD	2
	A. Right-of-Way	2
	B. Keep to the Right	2
	C. Passing	3
	D. Turning	4
	E. A Place to Park	5
III.	GUIDE POSTS	5
	A. Traffic Signs	5
	B. Pavement Markings	6
	C. Traffic Signals	7
IV.	SENSIBLE DRIVING	8
	A. Safe Driving	8
V.	OTHER ROAD CITIZENS	10
	A. Pedestrians	10
VI.	IN CASE OF ACCIDENT	11
	A. If you are involved	11
	B. If you are first at the scene	13
VII.	SUMMARY OF BASIC DRIVER'S RULES	13
VIII.	SUMMARY OF DRIVING SKILLS	16

BASIC FUNDAMENTALS OF DRIVING

I. **WHAT TO WATCH OUT FOR IN YOUR VEHICLE**

   A. BRAKES
   Brakes become worn and the linings must be replaced. Oil or grease may seep in and cause slipping or binding. Water may set in during wet weather. Dirt from dusty roads may filter in and make them grab. They may get out of adjustment and not apply evenly to all wheels. (You can test this by stopping your car suddenly on a level, hard-surfaced road. If your car pulls in one direction or another, adjustment is needed. But make this test only at a slow speed when no other cars are nearby.) If your car has hydraulic brakes, have the fluid checked frequently to maintain the proper amount in the system. Constant loss of fluid or the brake pedal going down too far indicates a leak in the system which should be repaired immediately. If you have four-wheel brakes, you must be able to stop after applying the brakes within 30 feet at 20 miles per hour, 67 feet at 30 miles per hour, 120 feet at 40 miles per hour, and 190 feet at 50 miles per hour.

   B. TIRES
   It is extremely dangerous to use tires after tread is worn off or if the sidewalls have been cut or slashed. Make certain they are inflated to the recommended pressure to take advantage of their safety factors. If a tire blows out, take your foot off the accelerator and hold the steering wheel as steadily as possible. Do not disengage your clutch or use your brakes until speed has been reduced considerably.
   　Danger Signs: If your car wanders or steers hard, or if your tires are smooth or worn unevenly, or if there is a "break" in the sidewall, have the tires checked immediately.

   C. STEERING
   Proper steering is essential for safe driving. If the front end of your car shakes or shimmies, or if your steering wheel has excessive "play" it seems to turn farther than usual before the front wheels react to your turn) or if the mechanism doesn't respond normally to your steering, you should have the steering mechanism checked immediately.

   D. LIGHTS
   You need all the light you can get, within the limits set by law, in order to see as far ahead as possible at night. For your protection, keep headlights at top efficiency, aimed properly, and replace them as they grow dim or burn out. Carry a box of extra fuses for replacement in an emergency. Each time you drive at night, first walk around your car to be sure your lights are working properly.

   E. WINDSHIELD
   Your windshield should be kept clean of dirt in summer and snow or ice in winter. It should be free of discoloration and pockmarks. Stickers, except those authorized by the Commissioner of Motor Vehicles, may not be used on front or back windows.

F. WIPERS
Your windshield wiper should be in good operating condition at all times. You should replace blades frequently.

G. MIRRORS
All cars must have rear view mirrors. These should be adjusted to give you a clear view of the road behind you.

H. WHEEL ALIGNMENT
At least once a year have your wheel alignment checked. Poor alignment can reduce tire life and cause excessive wear, looseness, and failure of the king pins as well as the components of the independent front wheel suspension system and tie rod ends. Such a condition is expensive to repair and is extremely dangerous in operating the vehicle.

II. **RULES OF THE ROAD**

A. RIGHT-OF WAY
The "right" in "right-of-way" is the key to most situations you will come across when reaching intersections. In general, the vehicle on your right has the privilege of proceeding before you do.
Exceptions: There are several situations when the general rule does not apply. They are:
1. When you approach an intersection, yield the right-of-way to a vehicle coming from the opposite direction which is within the intersection or so close as to be an immediate hazard. Other vehicles coming from the opposite direction must yield the right-of-way to you, if you already are in the intersection. This rule does not apply when both vehicles are halted outside of the intersection and both are to start at the same time. In this case, the car going straight ahead has the right-of-way.
2. If you notice an approaching fire engine, ambulance, or other emergency vehicle displaying a red light and an audible signal, you must yield right-of-way to that vehicle and immediately drive to a position parallel to, and as close as possible to, the right-hand edge or curb of the roadway and stop until the emergency vehicle has passed. On a one-way road, three or more lanes in width, you may drive to either edge or curb and halt. You must keep clear of intersections.
3. If you are about to enter or cross a highway from a private road or driveway, you must yield the right-of-way to all vehicles on the highway.
4. You must give the right-of-way to pedestrians in crosswalks.
Remember: The right-of-way is easy to give another driver. It doesn't cost you a penny. But it may cost your life if you try to grab it even when it is rightfully yours and the other fellow is taking it away.

B. KEEP TO THE RIGHT
The Safe Way: Driving on the wrong side of the road is one of the major causes of accidents. Your failure to keep on your own side may not get you into an accident, but may force the other driver off the road or cause him to lose control while avoiding you.

Keep to the Right: In the United States and Canada, traffic drives on the right-hand side of the road in most circumstances

Exceptions: There are several situations where this rule does not apply. They are:
1. When overtaking and passing another vehicle proceeding in the same direction as you are.
2. When passing pedestrians, animals, or obstructions in the right lane.
3. When you are on a road, or certain lanes of it, marked for one-way traffic.

Musts: You must stay on the right-hand side of the road in these situations:
1. When you are approaching the crest of a hill.
2. When you are approaching a curve and you cannot see around it.
3. When you are within 100 feet of a railroad grade crossing.
4. When your view is obstructed and you are within 100 feet of a bridge, viaduct, or tunnel.
5. When you are traveling slowly, in comparison with other traffic.
6. Do not speed up when other vehicles start to pass you.
7. When pavement markings prohibit driving on the left.

C. PASSING

Pass on the Left: The general rule is to pass other vehicles going in the same direction as you are on the left, allowing plenty of distance to clear the overtaken vehicle. Never pass unless you are sure you have enough time and space to get back in line. You must return to the right lane as soon as practical and safe. And signal before you pass and before you return to the right-hand lane, either with your hand or mechanical turn signals.

Exceptions: You may pass on the right under certain limited circumstances, so long as you do not drive off the pavement. These are:
1. When the vehicle ahead is making a left turn.
2. When you are traveling on a one-way road wide enough for two cars, provided such passing is not forbidden by signs.
3. When you are traveling on a road with unobstructed pavement and room for two or more lanes of traffic in each direction, provided such passing is not forbidden by signs.

Don't Pass: Passing is forbidden in certain circumstances. These include:
1. You may not pass a vehicle stopped at a crosswalk to allow a pedestrian to cross.
2. You may not pass from either direction a school bus which has halted to load or unload passengers, even when the highway is divided by a center mall. Such vehicles are marked "School Bus," and will have red lights flashing. You must stop before reaching the bus and wait for the bus to start, unless you are waved on by the driver or a police officer.

Tips on Passing: Danger is always present when you pass another vehicle. Always be sure any vehicles behind you are not attempting to pass, and that cars from the opposite direction are far enough away so you won't get involved in a difficult traffic situation. Don't cut back into the right-hand lane too quickly and risk hitting the overtaken car.

When a Car Passes You: Stay to your right as far as possible without going off the pavement and slow up slightly. Be alert if the other driver cuts back too quickly.

D. TURNING

Make Your Intentions Known: The first thing to do when changing directions or turning is to look around and behind your car. Be sure that you have an unobstructed path for the turn you are about to make. All turns should be made with caution and reduced speed. Let the other drivers know your intentions. Your car is probably equipped with mechanical turn signals, and you must use them or the recommended arm signals for at least 100 feet before you make your turn. Always be sure your mechanical signals are switched off after the turn as been completed.

Hand Signals: The prescribed hand signals, which you may wish to use, are:
- Left Turn: Arm and hand extended horizontally;
- Right Turn: Hand and arm extended upward with arm folded in right angle at the elbow;
- Slow or Stop: Hand and arm extended downward.

Making Right Turn: Both the approach and the turn should be made as close as practicable to the right-hand curb or edge of the road.

Left Turn on Two-Way Road: Approach the turn with your left wheels as close to the center line of the road as possible. After entering the intersection, make the left turn so that you keep to the left of the center of intersection and leave the intersection to the right of the center of the road you are entering.

Left Turn From Two-Way Road into One-Way Road: Approach the turn with your left wheels close to the center line of the road. Turn before reaching the center of the intersection and leave the intersection to the right of the center of the road you are entering.

Left Turn From One-Way Road into One-Way Road: Approach the turn in the left lane. After entering the intersection, turn so as to leave the intersection as nearly as possible in the left-hand lane of the road you are entering.

On Any Left Turn into Approaching Traffic: If oncoming traffic prevents you from making the turn as soon as you reach the intersection, do not wait behind edge of crosswalk. Proceed into the intersection and wait there for traffic to clear so that you may complete your turn. Traffic behind you can then often proceed on your right.

Right Turn: Approach the turn as far to the right as possible, and make the turn as close as possible to the right curb or edge of the road.

Left Turn From One-Way Road into Two-Way Road: Approach the turn in the left lane. Make the turn to the left of the center of the intersection and leave the intersection to the right of the center of the road you are entering.

Left Turn From a One-Way Road into One-Way Road: Approach the turn in the left lane. After entering the intersection, turn so as to leave the intersection as nearly as possible in the left-hand lane of the road you are entering.

Left Turn From Two-Way Road into Two-Way Road: Approach the turn with your left wheels as close as possible to the center line of the road. After entering the intersection, make the left turn, when possible, to the left of the center of the intersection. (Old law required vehicles to pass to the right of the center of the road.) the left turn has to be made so that you leave the intersection to the right of the center of the road you are entering.

Left Turn From Two-Way Road into One-Way Road: Approach the turn with your left wheels as close to the center line of the road as possible. Make the turn before

reaching the center of the intersection and leave the intersection as nearly as possible in the left-hand lane of the road you are entering.
Left Turn: Hand and arm extended horizontally.
Right Turn: Hand and arm extended upward.
Stop or Decrease Speed: Hand and arm extended downward.

E. A PLACE TO PARK
Why Parking is Limited: Parking is regulated and sometimes forbidden in certain locations. Usually this is done as a safety measure, and to allow rapid, smooth flow of traffic.
"No Parking" Signs: These mean that you may stop a vehicle in that space only temporarily to actually load or unload merchandise or passengers.
"No Stopping" Signs: These mean you may not stop a vehicle in that space for any purpose except when necessary to avoid conflict with other traffic or in compliance with the directions of a police officer.
"No Standing" Signs: These mean you may stop a vehicle in that space only temporarily to actually receive or discharge passengers.
No Stopping Here:
1. On a Sidewalk: In front of a driveway.
2. On a Crosswalk: Alongside or opposite any road excavation or obstruction.
3. On the road side of a parked vehicle.
No Stopping Here Either:
1. Within an intersection unless permitted by signs or parking meters.
2. Within 15 feet of a fire hydrant (unless a different distance is indicated by a sign), except when a licensed operator is in the front seat who can move the vehicle in case of emergency.
No Standing Here: Unless indicated otherwise by signs or parking meters:
1. Within 10 feet of a crosswalk at an intersection.
2. Within 30 feet on the approach to a traffic signal or "stop" sign at the side of the roadway.
3. Between a safety zone and the curb.
4. Within 50 feet of a railroad crossing.
5. On a bridge or in a tunnel.
Parallel Parking: Except where angle parking is permitted, you must park parallel where there are curbs—wheels within 12 inches of the curb. On two-way roads, you should park, stand or stop with the right wheels parallel to the right-hand curb; on one-way roads parallel to nearest curb.

For Safety's Sake: For the safety of your car and the safety of others, never park where it will be a hazard to traffic.

III. **GUIDE POSTS**

A. TRAFFIC SIGNS
Special Meanings: State highway signs have special shapes and colors, and these shapes and colors have special meanings for drivers. Red and white, black and white, yellow and black, or white and green are used in places where danger exists. They indicate the particular danger ahead.

Stop: This is an eight-sided sign with a red background. It means you must come to a full stop at a stop line if one is marked on the highway. If there is none, then stop at the crosswalk. If there is neither a stop line nor a crosswalk, stop at the point nearest the intersecting road where you can see approaching traffic in both directions. Proceed with caution after yielding the right-of-way to any vehicle which has entered the intersection from another road or which is so close as to be an "immediate hazard." (The older yellow "Stop" signs have the same meaning.)

Railroad: This is a round sign containing an "X" and the letters "RR" on a yellow background. It means you are approaching a railroad crossing. Buses and certain trucks must stop at grade crossings; other vehicles must use caution.

Yield Right-of-Way: Relatively new on many state highways, this sign varies slightly in shape from an inverted pyramid and in wording, but one word, "YIELD" always appears on it. It may say "Yield Right-of-Way" or just "Yield" and it may be white or black letters on a red or yellow background, but in any case it means you should approach such a sign with caution. A complete stop is not required unless there is traffic on the intersecting road. You must give the other traffic the right-of-way.

Other Signs: Diamond-shaped signs tell you of permanent physical hazards such as curves, steep hills, or narrow bridges. Rectangular signs are used to post regulations and to warn of possible operating hazards.

B. PAVEMENT MARKINGS

Lines and Lanes: State highways are marked with white or yellow lines. Each of these lines has a meaning of its own. Here is what the markings mean:

1. Broken Line: This line defines traffic lanes. You may cross it if crossing will not interfere with traffic.
2. Solid Line: Separates opposing traffic lanes. You should keep to the right of it, but may cross it if conditions permit, unless this is forbidden by local ordinance. Be especially cautious in crossing this line, however.
3. Solid and Broken Double Line: If the broken line is on your side, you may cross if traffic permits. If the solid line is on your side, you may cross except for a left turn from or into a road or driveway.
4. Double Solid Line: You should never cross this line except to turn into or from a road or driveway.
5. Crosswalk Line: This line, usually at a right angle to the curb, designates the area in which a pedestrian always has the right of way, provided he is not crossing against a red light.
6. "Stop" Line: This is a line across a highway usually at right angles to the curb at an intersection. If a stop is required at the intersection, you should stop in back of the line. Make a full stop, and start up only when it is safe to do so.
7. Arrows: These are painted on some highways, especially where there are multiple lanes, to help guide into proper lanes.
8. Broken Line: Defines traffic lanes. You may cross it if crossing will not interfere with traffic.
9. Solid Line: Separates opposing traffic lanes. You should keep in line but you may cross it when conditions are favorable for you to do so. BE CAUTIOUS.

10. Solid and Broken Line: Do not cross from the solid line side of the road, except for turn from or into private roads. You may cross from the broken line side, exercising EXTREME CAUTION.
11. Double Solid Line: No crossing allowed except for left turn from or into private roads.
12. Use of Double Line on Hills: The motorist often sees double line markings on a hill. A motorist on the right, who is climbing the hill, and who cannot see beyond the crest, is forbidden to start to pass by the solid line on his side, which he must not cross. A motorist coming down the hill can see a reasonable distance and is therefore free to use his judgment. Because the broken line is on his side, he may cross it if the road is clear ahead.
13. Reduction in Pavement Widths: The point at which a pavement narrows in width is dangerous because a lane which may be used by traffic on the wide pavement, disappears on the narrow pavement. To avoid confusion, traffic in this lane is shunted to the right.

C. TRAFFIC SIGNALS

<u>Red, Green and Amber</u>: These are among the most effective traffic devices for preventing accidents and tie-ups at intersections. Here is what the standard red, green and yellow indications mean:

1. Green Alone: You may proceed through the intersection or make a turn, unless a sign prohibits such a turn. But you must yield the right of way to other vehicles and pedestrians lawfully within the intersection or an adjacent crosswalk at the time the light changed.
2. Steady Yellow Alone: This warns you that the red signal will follow immediately, and that you may not enter or still be crossing the intersection when the signal turns red.
3. Steady Red Alone: This means stop before entering the intersection or one of its crosswalks. You must wait for the green light or arrow. The same rules apply here as for a stop sign as to where you should stop.
4. Dark Period, or Red-Green Combined When Shown Following Green: This period, on two-color signals, warns you that the red signal will follow immediately and that you may not enter the intersection after the signal turns red.
5. Steady Red With Green Arrow, Steady Yellow With Green Arrow, or Green Arrow Alone: This means you may, with caution, enter the intersection only to move in the direction indicated by the arrow. You must yield the right of way to pedestrians lawfully within a crosswalk and to other traffic lawfully using the intersection.
6. Flashing Red Signal: This means stop before the nearest crosswalk or limit line. If there is no such line, stop before entering the intersection. Proceed after yielding the right-of-way to any vehicle which has entered the intersection from another road or which is so close as to be an immediate hazard. This signal has the same meaning as a "stop" sign, and you should stop at the same place as for that type of sign.
7. Flashing Yellow Signal: This means you may proceed with caution.
8. When a Traffic Officer is Directing: Regardless of what the signal tells you to do, you should obey the officer's directions.

IV. SENSIBLE DRIVING

Good sense and good driving go hand in hand.

Rules that apply to our general conduct apply as well on the road. Yet every year, hundreds of people are killed and thousands of others are injured because they didn't use good sense. Being sensible and being alert go hand in hand. The first general rule of sensible driving is to keep alert, with your eyes on the road at all times. Here are a few other rules to help you drive sensibly. If you follow them, driving will be safer and easier for you.

A. SAFE DRIVING

<u>Night Driving</u>: The night hours between dusk and dawn are, by far, the most dangerous time to be on the highway. To protect yourself when it is dark out, you should follow these rules:
1. Your headlights must be turned on one half-hour after sunset until one half-hour b before sunrise.
2. Switch your headlights to low beam when an oncoming vehicle is within 500 feet, or when a vehicle you are overtaking is within 200 feet.
3. Drive more slowly. The distance you can see is shortened, even with properly adjusted headlights. Always be sure you can stop within the distance lighted by your headlight—350 feet or approximately 21 car lengths.
4. Be sure your taillight is working properly. It must be visible for 500 feet from the back of your car.
5. If you park your car at night, always be sure it is completely off the road. If you leave it facing traffic, keep your parking lights lighted.
6. Pedestrians who carry no lights never seem to realize how hard it is for you to see them after dark. Bad visibility carries no weight in court as an excuse for a pedestrian accident. Watch out for pedestrians.
7. Fix your eyes on the right-hand side of the road when passing an oncoming car at night. This will show you how far to the right you may go, and it also will help minimize the glare. There is always a second or two when you must drive blind past the oncoming car. Just before that brief period, slow down and try to get an impression of what is ahead, so you can drive from memory for that second or two when you are blinded.

<u>Alcohol and Gasoline</u>: No one knows for sure how many automobile accidents are caused each year by mixing drinking and driving. But a recent survey showed that in 62 percent of fatal accidents, alcohol was at least a factor.

It is dangerous to drink and drive. You may think you hold your drinks pretty well. But medical studies show that, under certain circumstances, one glass of beer or one cocktail is enough to impair your judgment. And when your judgment is impaired, you will take chances you would not normally take. When this happens, you are flirting with an accident.

How much can you safely drink and then drive? The amount varies, not only with the individual, but with other factors such as when he last ate.

The only safe rule is this: If you have had even as little as a single drink, then it is wise to let someone else do the driving. But under no circumstances should you permit yourself to drive if there is any possibility your judgment has suffered in the slightest as the result of drinking.

Doors: It is just plain good sense to be especially careful when getting out of your car. When you park by a curb, you may leave or enter your car from the left side only when no traffic is approaching. By the same token, when you see a parked car ahead always be prepared to handle the situation if an unthinking occupant should open his left door suddenly.

Keys in Car: When you leave your car unattended, you must stop the motor, lock the ignition, remove the key, and set the brakes. If you leave your keys in an unattended vehicle, you commit a traffic infraction.

Litterbugs: Not only is untidiness bad manners, it is also illegal and dangerous. Carelessly throwing refuse from your car can result in a fine (for first offense) of up to $50. Besides, the paper could blow into another car or against the windshield and confuse or temporarily blind the driver, causing an accident.

Tailgating (Following Too Closely): You never can be absolutely sure what the car ahead will do. To give yourself plenty of space to stop in time, follow this simple rule: Allow at least one car length between your car and the one ahead for each ten miles of speed. At 20 miles an hour, allow two car lengths; at 60, allow at least six car lengths. You should also take into consideration the amount of traffic and especially the condition of the road surface. Also, you may not follow any fire apparatus on its way to a fire by closer than 200 feet in a city or 500 feet in rural areas.

Coasting: The motor of your car helps you keep the speed under control. But it can only do so when the car is "in gear." Thus, when you coast or drive with the car in neutral gear, you are losing needed control.

Overcrowding: The law forbids more than three persons in the front seat of your car. More specifically, it says that the front seat shall not be so crowded that the passengers obstruct the driver's view or interfere with his control over the mechanism. If your car is small, then sometimes even three in the front seat is too many.

Horns: Nobody likes a loud-mouth, and a driver who constantly toots his horn is the loud-mouth of the road. Horns are to be used when passing other cars, or as a warning, but not otherwise.

Hitch-Hiking: It may seem the neighborly thing to do if you pick up a hitch-hiker. But not only are you taking a chance on the character of the hitchhiker; you also are posing a traffic hazard by suddenly stopping to pick him up. The picking up of hitch-hikers is not recommended. Hitchhiking itself is against the law.

Monoxide Gas: The exhaust from your car is highly poisonous. If your car is not properly sealed, there is danger of the fumes seeping in and killing you. So always drive with a window open wide enough to allow proper ventilation, even in the coldest or wettest weather.

Fatigue: When you are tired, it is dangerous to drive. Sometimes the monotony of driving can tire you. If this is the case, simply pulling off to the side of the road and getting out to stretch and rest your eyes a few minutes will help you. At other times, it is better to pull off and sleep for an hour or two. Accident records are filled with cases of overtired drivers who thought they could stay awake another hour or two—and could not.

Speeding: Besides being illegal, speeding is one of the most dangerous of all traffic violations. A surprisingly high percentage of accidents, especially fatal accidents, result from this offense. Maximum speed limit is 50 miles an hour unless otherwise posted. In addition, certain areas are designated for speeds below. Thus when you see a posted speed limit, you can be sure it is a realistic limit, and you should govern yourself accordingly. Furthermore, the legal speed limit is not necessarily the safe speed. Many factors, such as traffic volume, or bad weather, may call for lower speed.

<u>Seat Belts</u>: Research studies have proved that in case of an accident, you are much safer from injury or possible death if you are wearing a seat belt.

<u>Children and Pets</u>: It is extremely dangerous to allow pets or small children to ride in the front seat of a car, where they may distract the driver. Children should be encouraged to "sit back in the seat," where they are less likely to bump their heads in case of a sudden stop. Seat belts are especially helpful for children.

<u>Winter Driving</u>: You need special equipment, such as snow tires or reinforced tire chains for winter driving. Windows should be kept clear of snow and ice. If it is slippery, test your stopping distance where there is no traffic, to give yourself an idea of how much space you need to stop. Be particularly careful at curves, hills, and intersections. Pump your brakes one, two, or more times a second to stop on slippery roads, rather than simply pressing down on the brake pedal.

<u>Other Bad Weather</u>: Rain reduces your visibility and ability to stop quickly. High speeds when it is extremely windy can result in loss of control. The best rule to follow is to keep your speed down—you should never drive faster than weather and road conditions permit. In dense fog, you should reduce speed and use the low beam of your headlights.

<u>At Intersections</u>: If traffic ahead is blocked so that you cannot clear the intersection, stop before you enter the intersection.

<u>Negotiating Curves</u>: To guide your car on a curve in the highway, you should enter such curve at reduced speed, accelerating slightly as you round it.

<u>Skidding</u>: Should your car be thrown into a skid, you may regain a straight path by turning your front wheels in the direction of the skid. Never apply the brakes hard, but lift your foot from the accelerator.

<u>Off the Pavement</u>: Should your right wheels drop off the pavement, slow down immediately and turn your front wheels sharply to the left until all four are back on the pavement.

V. OTHER ROAD CITIZENS

   A. PEDESTRIANS

<u>Crossing on Signal</u>: Pedestrians may cross a road, being sure to stay within the crosswalk, on a green signal. They may not cross it facing a "wait" or "don't walk" signal, nor may they cross on the red or yellow signal or the red-green combined or dark period following a green signal unless facing a "walk" signal. On a green arrow, whether alone or accompanied by a steady red or yellow, the pedestrian may enter the road only if he can do so safely and without interfering with vehicle traffic.

<u>Intersections Without Signal</u>: When there are no traffic signals or if they are not operating, drivers must yield the right-of-way, slowing or stopping if necessary, for a pedestrian crossing within a crosswalk.

<u>Crossing Between Intersections</u>: A pedestrian crossing the road between intersections, except at a marked crosswalk, must yield the right-of-way to all vehicles

on the road. Pedestrians crossing a road where a pedestrian tunnel or overhead crossing has been provided must also yield the right-of-way to vehicles.

Walking on the Road: It is unlawful for pedestrians to walk in the road where there are sidewalks. Where there are no sidewalks, a pedestrian must walk on the left side of the road or its shoulder facing the traffic, and move as far to the left as possible when a vehicle approaches. Two or more pedestrians should walk in single file and never abreast of each other.

Tipsy Pedestrians: Research has shown that many pedestrians killed by automobiles have been drinking. Such pedestrians do foolish things, and, what is worse, they often do them at night when the driver has less chance of seeing them. As a driver, you must realize that such pedestrians may be unreasonable, but since they have so little chance to survive a collision with your car, you must protect them.

Bus Stops: Remember that pedestrians leaving buses may be confused as to direction, so always watch out for them. And be sure to stop when overtaking or meeting a standing school bus which is taking on or discharging passengers or displaying flashlight lights.

Blind Pedestrians: You must be especially careful when encountering blind persons. The law requires drivers at or near intersections to grant the right-of-way to blind pedestrians. Under the so-called "White Cane Law" you must yield the right-of-way to pedestrians who are crossing or attempting to cross a highway and who are guided by seeing-eye dogs or who are carrying, in a raised position, a white or metallic cane, or a white cane with a red tip.

White Clothes: Pedestrians should bear in mind that part of the responsibility for their safety rests on themselves as well as the driver. At night a pedestrian should wear light-colored clothes so the driver can see him better.

VI. IN CASE OF ACCIDENT

No matter how carefully you drive, you may become involved in a motor vehicle accident. There are a number of things you should do, and some you MUST do, in this eventuality. In the interest of humanity, you are called upon to give whatever assistance you can to the injured. In the interest of preventing similar accidents in the future, you are required to make a report to the Department of Motor Vehicles on how the accident occurred, where, at what time of day, the condition of the weather and of the street or highway, and other pertinent data.

A. IF YOU ARE INVOLVED

Stop: Perhaps your car is damaged severely and cannot proceed, or maybe the harm is only slight. Nevertheless, you are to stop immediately.

At Night: If an accident occurs at night or on a heavily-travelled street or highway, or where your car cannot be readily seen by approaching vehicles, move it off the highway immediately if possible. Leave your parking lights on.

Injuries: First, see if anyone has been injured, and give whatever assistance you can. If the injuries are serious, do not attempt to move the person, but try to get medical help as quickly as possible.

Information: If you are not hurt, make your name and address, license and registration number and name of your insurance company known to the operator of the other car (and to any officer). At the same time, obtain the other operator's name, address, license number and name of his insurance company and write it down. In case of a pedestrian, get his full name and address, if possible.

Report to Police: Even if the other party on the accident is unable to take your name and address, report to the nearest police station as soon as you can. The police will show you how to make out your report of the accident on the forms which are provided by the Department of Motor Vehicle.

If You Are Hurt: If you are unable to make a report to the Department of Motor Vehicles within 48 hours, as the law requires, get some passenger, member of the family, a friend or your doctor to send the report in for you. Report forms are available at all police stations, courts, or branch offices of the Department.

Unattended Vehicles: You also must report any accident in which you collide with an unattended vehicle or other property. Find the owner and give him your name and address, or report to the nearest police station.

What Accidents to Report: Any accident which involves personal injury or death or property damage in excess of $1,000 must be reported to the Department of Motor Vehicles within 48 hours. Accident report blanks may be obtained at any police station, Department of Motor Vehicles office or Motor Vehicle section of a County Clerk's Office.

Animals: If your car hits and injures a horse, a dog, or cattle, you must stop and report the accident to the owner, is possible, or to a police official, and see that the animal gets necessary attention. Wild and domestic animals are entitled to humane treatment.

Penalties: Always remember this: If you fail to stop your car after an accident, if you fail to report and make yourself known to the other driver or a police official, or if you fail to fulfill any of the other requirements in this section, you may lose your license and face criminal court action for leaving the scene of an accident.

Conscience: On top of those penalties, your conscience will always bother you, if by your failure to observe the rules of conduct someone dies or suffers needlessly.

Submersion: If your car goes into deep water—do not panic. If it dips below the surface with the wheels down, the best escape technique is through the open windows before the water reaches window level. If it sinks too rapidly for you to escape while it is at the surface, climb into the rear seat. A pocket of air will form there and will give you time to plan your way out. You can open the nearest window or wait until the pressure of the water inside is equal to that outside and then open a door.

Moral Responsibility: Suppose you come upon the scene of an accident in which the car ahead of you has smashed into some object or has skidded and overturned. Do you:

1. Drive as closely as you can to the crash?
2. Try to haul people out of the wreckage?
3. Speed past and let someone else be the Good Samaritan?

Sounds ridiculous, doesn't it? But some people would, simply because they do not know any better or they do not want to get involved.

You owe it to yourself and to others to help all you can. For you might be in a position sometime of being the occupant of a car in an accident and will not be able to help yourself. So do the smart thing. Follow the common sense suggestions which are listed here; you may save a life or you may prevent further damage.

B. IF YOU ARE FIRST AT THE SCENE
<u>Stop</u>: Get your car off the road far enough away from the wreck to protect it from other traffic. Then as calmly as possible decide what to do.
<u>Warn Traffic</u>: Find some way or get some other person's help to warn or stop approaching traffic if necessary to prevent other crashes. Ask others to go for help, either to the nearest telephone or the nearest police officer. Warn traffic coming from both directions far enough from the scene so that cars nearing the accident will slow down in plenty of time.
<u>Turn Off Ignition</u>: As soon as possible, get to the wreck and turn off the ignition to prevent fire if it has not already started. If a fire does not start right away, the chances are it will not, and you can relax somewhat. If it has, however, get the people out as quickly as possible and as far away as possible in the event there is an explosion.
<u>Helping the Injured</u>: If there are injured persons in the car or lying on the ground nearby after being thrown out and there is no fire, don't move them. Make sure they are protected from traffic and covered with coats or blankets to keep them warm. Without trying to move them, loosen collar, ties, and belts to help them breathe easier. Unless you are skilled in first aid, however, do not try to treat their injuries before medical assistance arrives except to try to stop any bleeding. You may make their hurts worse.
<u>If Someone is Pinned</u>: If the wreck is overturned with someone underneath, don't try to lift the car unless you have enough strong persons to do it, and then not until you are sure no one will be crushed under the other side. Police, highway patrolmen and emergency truck operators are skilled in dealing with accidents. Unless you know what you are doing, leave it to them.
<u>Make Yourself Known</u>: After you have done what you can to assist the injured, give your name and address to the police. Since you may have seen the accident occur, your eyewitness account may be of help to them.
<u>If You Are Not There First</u>: Don't be curious. If you are not asked to stop and lend your assistance, move on so as not to cause a possible traffic jam and further accidents. Many drivers slow down or stop to rubberneck at the accident scene, thereby neglecting their driving.

VII. SUMMARY OF BASIC DRIVER'S RULES

A. OBJECTIVES
1. Be alert; concentrate on your driving whenever you operate a vehicle.

B. SPEED
2. You shall continuously maintain your vehicle under such control so as to be able to bring it to a complete stop within the assured clear distance ahead.
3. You shall not operate a vehicle at a speed greater than is reasonable and proper having due regard to weather, visibility, traffic, intersections, width and character of roadway, type, condition and loading of the vehicle, your own alertness, and any existing condition affecting your ability to stop before collision.
4. You shall not drive in any state, county, city, municipality, or area under the control of the Federal Government at a speed greater than that permitted by the

authorities in those areas. All personnel shall follow rules and regulations laid down by the Bureaus in which they are employed.

5. When meeting or overtaking a school bus, which has stopped to load or unload passengers, you shall stop and proceed only when the bus is in motion.
6. You shall approach a railroad crossing or drawbridge at such a speed as to permit stopping should danger of collision require and shall proceed only if the way is clear. (Exception: See Rule 39 for buses and trucks transporting personnel.)

C. RIGHT-OF-WAY
7. You shall give the right-of-way when required by signs, traffic lights or signals from authorized individuals, always coming to a full stop at a STOP sign.
8. You shall give the right-of-way to all vehicles on a main highway or thoroughfare which you intend to enter or cross.
9. You shall give the right-of-way to every pedestrian unless he clearly indicates that he is giving it to you.
10. At unmarked intersections you shall give the right-of-way to vehicles approaching from your right, and to those which entered the intersection before you.
11. You shall give the right-of-way to a vehicle making a left turn across your path if it has started to turn before you reach the intersection.
12. You shall give the right-of-way to emergency vehicles, such as police car, firetrucks, and ambulances.
13. You shall give the right-of-way to persons on bicycles.

D. OVERTAKING AND PASSING
14. You shall not attempt to pass another vehicle proceeding in the same direction on curves or hills unless you have at least 500 feet of unobscured vision.
15. Do not attempt to pass before checking your left side and rear view mirrors for danger.
16. When driving in heavy traffic, with several lanes moving in the same direction, you shall stay in your own lane and proceed at its pace, except when changing lanes in preparation for a turn.
17. You shall not recklessly move into the right lane from a lane which has stopped apparently for left turns.
18. You shall not pass at intersections.
19. You shall allow an overtaking vehicle to pass you safely.

E. SLOWING, STOPPING, TURNING, BACKING
20. You shall test the brakes of your vehicle before departing from your station.
21. Unless it is unavoidable, you shall not stop suddenly.
22. Maintain a reasonable distance, depending upon speed and driving conditions, between your vehicle and a vehicle ahead of you.
23. Make turns at intersections only from the proper lane.
24. Before baking you shall survey the area to ascertain that it is clear and suitable.

F. SIGNALS
   25. You shall always clearly indicate your intention to stop, change lanes or turn at intersections by signaling.

G. NIGHT DRIVING
   26. Always use extra caution when driving at night.
   27. Display your lights from one-half hour after sunset to one-half hour before sunrise and whenever else poor visibility demands them.

H. USE OF SEAT BELTS
   28. All front-seat passengers and all children must have seat belts fastened whenever the vehicle is in motion.

I. TRAFFIC AIDS: LIGHTS, SIGNS, AND MARKINGS
   29. You shall obey all applicable traffic signs and signals.

J. WEATHER AND ROADS
   30. Limit the operation of vehicles to a bare minimum in inclement weather.

K. HILLS
   31. You shall not drive downgrade with your gears in neutral or your clutch disengaged.

L. PARKING
   32. You shall park properly and safely at proper places.
   33. You shall secure your vehicle to avoid its movement while unoccupied or its use by an unauthorized person.
   34. You shall always check traffic flow before leaving a parking space to enter any thoroughfare.

M. USE OF VEHICLES
   35. You shall not operate a vehicle unless you have in your possession a personal motor vehicle operator's identification card.
   36. You shall not remove your vehicle from your station without proper authorization.
   37. You shall not permit unauthorized persons to ride in your vehicle.
   38. You shall not operate a vehicle when you are physically unfit from any cause.

N. BUSES, TRUCKS, AND EMERGENCY VEHICLES
   39. Upon approaching a railroad crossing when transporting personnel in a bus or truck, you shall bring your vehicle to a full stop not less than 10 feet nor more than 50 feet from the rails and shall not proceed until you have ascertained that the crossing is clear.
   40. When transporting personnel in the bed of a truck, you shall not exceed a speed of 30 miles per hour.
   41. Buses or other vehicles carrying eight or more passengers shall be operated only by persons who are at least 21 years of age.

42. You shall take all necessary precautions to prevent the injury of personnel transported in trucks or buses.
43. When transporting personnel, you shall not load beyond capacity.
44. You shall not load your vehicle in a manner which will obscure your view ahead of to either side or in any way interfere with the safe operation of your vehicle.
45. Every trailer shall be coupled with suitable safety chains or cables to the towing vehicle.

VIII. SUMMARY OF DRIVING SKILLS

A. WHAT ARE THE MOST IMPORTANT SKILLS IN DRIVING?
There are two basic skills that are the most important.

One is called *tracking*. By this is meant the physical ability to drive a car from point A to point B.

The other is called *detection*. And that is often the hardest part. Being able to sense what is happening around you and detecting potentially dangerous situations.

To be a really good driver, you must master both. And that requires using *tracking* and *detection* at one time. It is not easy.

B. WHICH ARE MORE IMPORTANT—PHYSICAL OR MENTAL DRIVING SKILLS?
You really cannot separate the two. How fast you *react to* something on the road is often dependent on *when* you realize an action must be taken. The more vigilant you are about the task of driving, the more likely you will be to detect and respond quickly to a potential problem.

C. IS THERE ONE DRIVING TECHNIQUE THAT IS BETTER THAN OTHERS?
Defensive driving is the best technique.

To be a good defensive driver you have to be alert. And the more alert you are, the better you drive. A chauffeur once gave a good tip about defensive driving. He said that he builds a *moving oval* of space around his car. As he drives, he tries to position himself so that he has space all around. That way, he can move right or left, forward or backward, to avoid trouble. Traffic conditions make this difficult to do all the time. But when he has the chance, he does it, because he stays on the defensive.

D. WHAT IS THE CORRECT POSITION FOR YOUR HANDS ON THE STEERING WHEEL?
Many people are taught that the 10 o'clock and 2 o'clock positions are best. But an authority says the 9 o'clock and 3 o'clock positions are better. You have more control and your arms will be less likely to tire.

E. THE SPEED LIMIT IS ALWAYS A SAFE SPEED, TRUE OR FALSE?
False. Speed limits are set for the best driving conditions. Slow down in heavy traffic, darkness and bad weather. But remember, if you are on a freeway, do not go too slowly. That can be very dangerous. Concentrate on staying within the speed limit and "going with the flow."

F. ARE THERE ANY TRICKS TO KEEPING YOUR MIND ALERT WHILE DRIVING?
One way is to keep your body alert. Sit up straight in the seat. Your car will tell you how it is responding. But you have to listen with your body as well as your ears. When you turn a corner too swiftly, you will feel it first in your bottom and your legs.

If there is a handling problem, you will notice it first in your hands and your arms.

You should be comfortable while driving, but not so comfortable that you are not prepared for the signals your car can give you.

G. ANY TIPS ON MAKING TURNS AT BUSY INTERSECTIONS?
Here is a tip on what *not* to do. Don't be in such a hurry to turn left that you turn your wheels before you start to make your move. Leaving your wheels straight is a defensive technique. Why? Because if you are struck from the rear and your wheels are turned left, you will be knocked into the path of oncoming traffic.

When you are making any turn, stay in the same lane. Do not swing wide into a different lane. Besides, taking more road than you need, you could really be inviting disaster.

H. WHAT IS A SAFE FOLLOWING DISTANCE?
The familiar answer is at least one car length for every 10 miles per hour. But there is a better answer: *at least a two-second interval.* To use it, simply select an object along the roadside ahead. When the car in front of you passes it, start counting "one-thousand-one, one-thousand two…" You should finish "one-thousand-two" as you reach the object. If you reach the object first, you are too close.

I. HOW SHOULD YOU SHAKE A TAILGATER?
Don't hit your brakes and try to scare him out of his wits. He may not react quickly enough and plow right into you. *Don't* let him intimidate you into driving too fast. Gradually slow down and give him every opportunity to pass. If he is really in a hurry, he will go around you when you slow down.

J. HOW SHOULD YOU REACT WHEN PEOPLE CUT IN FRONT OF YOU?
You are following at a safe distance and someone cuts in front of you. You back off to a safe distance and someone cuts in front of you. You back off to a safe distance and someone does it again. What next?

The answer is to back off again. If you get frustrated and start following too closely, you are only increasing your chances of a possible rear-end collision. Keep a level head. Never let emotion get the best of you.

K. SO WHAT DOES IT TAKE TO BE A SKILLFUL DRIVER?
The three C's of driving are:

<u>Cooperation</u>: Competition has no place on the road. Be friendly and courteous. Help other drivers. You would want them to help you.

<u>Communication</u>: Don't isolate yourself. Let other drivers know what you plan to do. Use your signals.

<u>Concentration</u>: Perhaps the most important thing of all. Keep your mind on your driving. Remember that driving is a task. Be vigilant in your efforts to stay alert. A skillful driver is a safe driver.

L. DRIVER PLEDGE
   I will:
   1. be courteous to other drivers and cooperate with them by driving friendly;
   2. consider safety above all else;
   3. feel responsible for all who ride with me;
   4. remain calm and vigilant at the wheel;
   5. keep an especially watchful eye for pedestrians;
   6. try to help other drivers when they are in difficulty;
   7. remember that the roads belong to two-wheeled vehicles as well as cars;
   8. see that regular maintenance and safety inspections are performed on my car;
   9. not drive if under the influence of drugs or alcohol; and
   10. obey all traffic laws.

www.ingramcontent.com/pod-product-compliance
Lightning Source LLC
Chambersburg PA
CBHW082210300426
44117CB00016B/2739